Mathematics and Computing: Level 3
Software Systems & their Development

Block 1 Introduction to Java

Acknowledgements

The following software applications were used to produce Figure A.1 and Figure A.2:
The Open University's version of LearningWorks which is derived from LearningWorks 0.7 (and contains work that is copyright of ObjectShare, Inc.). Copyright © 1996-97, Adele Goldberg and Neometron, Inc. All rights reserved.

Borland JBuilder 3.5 Foundation

Borland Inprise Copyright 2000 Inprise Corporation

All rights reserved. All Inprise and Borland brands and product names are trademarks or registered trademarks of Inprise Corporation.

This publication forms part of the Open University course M301 *Software Systems and their Development*. Details of this and other Open University courses can be obtained from the Course Reservations Centre, PO Box 724, The Open University, Milton Keynes MK7 6ZS, United Kingdom: tel. +44 (0)1908 653231, e-mail ces-gen@open.ac.uk

Alternatively, you may visit the Open University web site at http://www.open.ac.uk where you can learn more about the wide range of courses and packs offered at all levels by the Open University.

To purchase this course or other components of Open University courses, contact Open University Worldwide Ltd, The Berrill Building, Walton Hall, Milton Keynes MK7 6AA, United Kingdom: tel. +44 (0)1908 858785; fax +44 (0)1908 858787; e-mail ouwenq@open.ac.uk; web site http://www.ouw.co.uk

The Open University, Walton Hall, Milton Keynes, MK7 6AA

First published 2000, second edition 2001, third edition 2002, fourth edition 2003

Edited, designed and typeset by The Open University.

Printed in the United Kingdom by The Charlesworth Group, Huddersfield

ISBN 0 7492 5786 5

4.1

Unit 1.1 Introduction and the IDE

CONTENTS

STUDY GUIDE

Aims

The aims of this unit are to:

- give an outline of the whole course and describe the purpose of each block;
- introduce some of the important issues in software development;
- introduce you to the facilities of the Java Integrated Development Environment (hereafter referred to as the IDE);
- examine some of the basic constructs of the Java programming language.

Materials required

For this unit you will require:

1 this course text;
2 *The 'Killer Robot' Case*;
3 the *Case Study*, Section 1;
4 the IDE;
5 the *IDE Handbook*;
6 Budd, Chapters 2 and 4.

Consult the web page for *Unit 1.1* from the M301 web site (http://M301.open.ac.uk) for access to the *Case Study*. Consult the web page, also, for access to *The 'Killer Robot' Case*, which is referred to on pages 4, 10 and 11 of this unit.

Budd, T. (2000) Understanding *Object-oriented Programming with Java*, second edition, Addison Wesley Longman (set book). ISBN 0-536-62310-4.

Required knowledge

Entry to this course assumes that you already know about the important concepts associated with Object-Oriented (OO) software development. It also assumes that you have programmed in an OO language. Before you begin work on this unit you should check your knowledge of OO concepts as suggested in the *Course Guide*. You should do the self-assessment test which can be found on the course web site. We shall henceforth assume that, if you had any trouble doing this test, you have subsequently studied the recommended reading to bring your knowledge up to the required level.

Programme of work

There are three sections to this unit. On the basis that an evening's work takes between 2½ and 3 hours to complete and that this unit should take five evenings to work through, including the completion of the TMA question associated with it, an estimated study plan is given in the following table.

[We recommend that you tackle the sections in the order they appear because the use of the IDE will reinforce the ideas introduced in the course text.]

Section	Number of evenings	Materials required
1	1	course text; *Case Study*, Section 1; *The 'Killer Robot' Case*; Budd, Chapter 2, Sections 2.1 and 2.2
2	2	course text; the IDE; *IDE Handbook*
3	2	course text; the IDE; *IDE Handbook*; Budd, Chapter 4; *The 'Killer Robot' Case*

Whenever you need to refer to other materials in the course, you will be given explicit instructions to do so. We have adopted the convention that such instructions will appear in a box, beginning with the one below.

> If you have not done so already, read the *Course Guide* where you will find important information about how the course is structured and suggestions on how you should make use of the various kinds of study materials in the course and, in particular, how you should use the SAQs and exercises.

Important note

There is a lot of material associated with this unit so it is vital that you use it wisely. Section 1 gives an introduction to the course and is not intended to be studied in depth. However, you must ensure that you read the background to the *Case Study* and the first few articles of *The 'Killer Robot' Case*, both of which can be accessed from the M301 web site. Do not spend more than an evening on this material at this stage.

Your primary goals for this unit are to become familiar with the IDE and to understand the basic constructs of the Java programming language introduced in Budd, Chapter 4.

1 INTRODUCTION TO THE COURSE

The aims of the course are to:

- enable you to read programs written in Java and to amend or extend existing software systems in response to new requirements, particularly in the area of networked systems;
- describe the major features of modern concurrent (distributed) systems;
- illustrate the use of the Unified Modelling Language in the analysis of new requirements in relation to existing solutions;
- analyse existing systems to identify their major architectural principles and software mechanisms, and to describe how they work both in isolation and together;
- introduce the development of software systems using an object-oriented approach with associated management practices.

By the end of the course you will be able to complete a realistic software development project. The software development project will form a case study that will be referred to throughout the course and will illustrate many of the concepts introduced in the course.

Block 1 of the course concentrates on building software components. It shows you the fundamentals of creating objects and building systems from them. We shall introduce you to the basics of Java as a means of illustrating the concepts involved.

The existence of communicating distributed software implies that there are separate sequential programs executing simultaneously (we use the term *concurrent processes* to describe such a situation). In Blocks 2 and 3 you will study the ramifications of concurrency in software systems. You can think of these blocks as providing the theoretical basis of distributed software.

Blocks 4 and 5 turn to the issues that arise in the process of developing software. These two blocks may be considered as providing the practice of software development.

Block 6 brings together the theory and practice, and provides you with the opportunity of putting what you have learned into practice via a small project based on a case study that you will have followed throughout the course.

The specific aim of the following subsections is to introduce the main topics of the course and to examine them in the context of the case study and a fictitious scenario. The scenario combines elements of software engineering and computer ethics, but also illustrates the complexities of software development.

1.1 Objectives

On completion of this section you should be able to:

1. describe the major issues associated with the development of large software systems;
2. list the important tools and mechanisms that are useful in developing such systems;
3. understand the role of each block of the course in tackling these issues and mechanisms.

1.2 Key terms and concepts

The important terms and concepts associated with this section are as follows.

abstraction
analysis
architecture
bridging software
business needs
CASE tools
client–server
component
concurrency
contract
design
distributed system
ethics
frameworks
HCI
Internet
legacy system
life cycle
maintenance
networking
pattern
plan
process
professional issues
programming
project management
quality assurance
requirements
security
software engineering
specification
testing
usability
validation
verification

1.3 Software development

M301 is about the development of software systems. In particular, it is concerned with software systems that are *large* (that is, much larger than can be comprehended by an individual at any one time) and *distributed* (that is, the software executes on geographically widely dispersed autonomous computer systems). Moreover, the development process takes place in an environment in which the majority of new software has to interact with existing systems.

Software development is a business activity

Software for large commercial and industrial applications, with which we shall be mainly concerned, is generally complex. Many firms rely on computers for the day-to-day running of their business and in some cases the software system *is* the business or forms a significant part of the business activity. That is, the business is critically dependent upon computer systems which, if they failed or went out of service for even a short time, could lead to the whole business collapsing. One implication of this is that changing, replacing or simply adding new functionality to existing software must be achieved without disruption to the business. Existing software systems that must be kept running are usually known as **legacy systems**. It is often the case that an enterprise has developed its activities in ways that were not envisaged when its legacy system was originally developed. The resulting software is often a collection of independent applications tied together with **bridging software**, that is, software specifically written so that two or more separate applications can work together. Thus, many systems consist of a number of applications, each individually complex, interacting with each other via complex bridging software.

The cost of developing and maintaining business software can be enormous and can form a large proportion of a firm's expenditure. It is now common to view software systems as *assets* because they are so expensive and so central to the business itself. Enterprises do not lightly undertake the complete replacement of such assets, which means that legacy systems of extreme age (in computing terms) continue to exist. Maintaining this kind of software can be very difficult and consequently expensive.

This description of the current state of software systems should convince you that there are severe problems facing software engineers in developing software. Much work in the field of *software engineering* is being devoted to finding ways of developing new software that will be maintainable into the future. Maintainability of software, either in terms of correcting faults or extending functionality, is just one of several qualities that good software should exhibit. Later in this course you will examine issues surrounding software quality and the techniques that are being adopted to ensure that quality is achieved.

Since software systems cannot at any given time be completely understood by a single individual, two facts emerge. First, software systems are developed as smaller separate elements that are designed to interact with other elements with ease (precisely what this means will be discussed later in the course). Second, software is often produced by teams of people working together to solve a particular problem. Thus, a good software engineer will not only have a good working knowledge of the field but will also have considerable skills in the area of team working. Errors and delays in projects are often due to human factors and not the result of the degree of difficulty of the problem being solved. Human factors loom large in the process of software development.

The software engineers, who are so important for success in software development, are themselves professionals. They must behave ethically and legally just as doctors are expected to behave ethically and legally. They may well belong to a professional society and are subject to standards set by that society.

Ultimately, software is developed to meet a (business) need. It is the responsibility of the software engineer to provide the required software. In a business setting, a contract exists between the customer and the developer for the provision of a product. The software specification will need to satisfy the customer's requirements. It will also enable the software developer to produce the required product. While the specification of the software will be the basis of the contract, there will be delivery dates and price constraints too.

Software development is an engineering discipline

Traditionally, software development has been studied and practised as a sequence of phases, and several phased approaches have been proposed. It is certainly true that the process starts by identifying what the 'user' wants from a particular piece of software. We have placed the term *user* in quotes because it is an overworked word and can represent a variety of roles. For example, when the need for a piece of software has been identified, who should be responsible for identifying what that software should do? Should it be a business executive who will ultimately be responsible for paying for the development? Should it be the person(s) (real user) who will interact with the software once it is built? Should it be others with the responsibility for examining business practices and recommending process change? Clearly, all these people must have a say, and ultimately, there should appear a **requirements specification** document which identifies (among other things) what the software should do (known as its functionality) and the environment in which it must work. Without a requirements specification, the developers will not know what is required to be developed and the business will not know what sort of product it is paying for.

In this course we shall use the term *customer* to refer to the person or business that wants a software system to be developed, and *user* (without quotes) to refer to the person who interacts with the software system when it is in use in the business context. The word *client* will be used in a technical sense to describe an item of software used in a particular role (as in, for example, a client–server architecture).

The process of generating the requirements specification is known as **analysis** because one is usually examining what the customer/user wants in terms of the business functions, that is, analysing the business in order to identify what the software should do. The analysis phase may be broken down into separate subphases. It begins with the elicitation of the requirements, that is, finding out what is required, followed by the specification of requirements, that is, the production of the requirements specification document. What is often interesting about the identification of requirements is that, as knowledge about the requirements increases, the requirements often change. Indeed, it is not uncommon for details to change throughout the whole of the software development process.

Following analysis and consideration of what needs to be developed, software engineers consider how to build it, by designing the software (a process called **design**) before coding it (often called **implementation**), testing it, and then delivering it to the customer. Ultimately, the software will cease to be useful and will be withdrawn from service. If we view the initial ideas as the birth of the system, and its final withdrawal as the death of the system we have a complete *life cycle* for the software.

No matter what method is used to develop the software, there will be a delivered product: the software.

Architecture and styles

Software is so complex and large that ways of thinking about it and describing it are needed. We talk about software *architecture*, borrowing this term from the building industry, though we do not mean to include the aesthetic element of building design, just the idea of taking an overview.

In order to be able to reason about the architecture, and feel confident that it will work successfully, we would like to build upon past successes. If possible the chosen architecture should be similar to a software system that has been built before, which can be called a standard design or **framework**. However, sometimes a system is unlike any existing system. For the parts that are being combined we would ideally like to be able to reuse software that has been built previously and tested in practice. Such a part is known as a **component**. If a part is unavailable, either an existing part will have to be adapted or a new one will have to be built. To build a new part involves identifying a sub-architecture composed of subparts, and so on. In developing a new architecture and its composition from existing parts, local design problems will have to be solved: parts will have to be arranged to achieve particular ends, and again tried and tested solutions can be drawn upon through *patterns*, which record good solutions from experienced designers.

If you wish, though it is not part of the course, you can obtain more information in R.T. Monroe, A. Kompanek, R. Melton and D. Garlan (1997) 'Architectural Styles, Design Patterns and Objects', *IEEE Software*, vol. 14, no. 1.

It is possible to recognize a number of *architectural styles* in software such as client-server. While these styles have not been given hard and fast definitions, they do convey to an experienced software engineer an overall picture of a software system. For example, in a client-server system you would expect to find two distinct kinds of software element: the client and the server, and there would typically be several instances of the client. You would also normally expect to find that such a system would be distributed, with each client and the server running on separate machines, such that a client makes requests to the server for some service. Notice that this description contains no application specific information; it has abstracted out application specific details.

In many ways, this is like describing the architecture of buildings: we can identify a variety of styles such as Roman, Gothic, Norman, and so on. Describing a specific building as Gothic tells you something about the overall style of the building, which is sufficient to distinguish it from other styles, but does not provide any information about the finer details. At a finer level of detail, you would expect a building in the Gothic style to have windows and doors built into frames with a pointed arch; and you would expect this pattern to be repeated throughout the building. In software, the notion of pattern is used in a similar way: it describes a particular kind of design at a finer level of detail than an architecture, but at a coarser level of detail than, for example, an individual class in an object-oriented design. An example of a software design pattern is the wrapper pattern. A **wrapper pattern** describes the situation in which an existing piece of software is 'encased' within a new piece of software. The additional piece of software provides a new interface to the old software, but the functionality of the whole is still provided by the old software. A wrapper may also provide additional functionality.

Describing the essential features of something and ignoring other details is a process often referred to as **abstraction**. Such an abstract description is known as a **model** or sometimes, confusingly, as an abstraction. The process of software development is often described as one of developing a succession of models, the final one being the software implementation. In the course of development one might assemble a collection of abstractions into another higher-level abstraction.

Quality and management

Software systems can be complex and large, and have to be developed by teams over several years. Systems are often critical for business success. This criticality means that the customer wants a system development process that is predictable — the facilities that the software system offers must be able to solve the customer's business problems, and the software must be delivered within a defined timescale and to an agreed budget.

Project management is needed to ensure that this will happen. This is common to all engineering enterprises in which the work required is broken down into smaller stages (or phases or activities), which are then broken down repeatedly into small tasks that can be accomplished by one person in a week to a month. The work has to be planned. This includes laying down the engineering processes that need to be carried out, determining what will happen and when, and defining the expected result that will be delivered at the end of each stage.

These plans will be created at the start of the project, perhaps detailing the first phase of work and only outlining the work thereafter. At the start of a project much of the detail about the required software may be uncertain, so detailed planning will be minimal. The plans will also include an estimate of the total work content and costs — but these may only be accurate to within 25% or so. The plans will need to be updated as the development process progresses, as more is learned about the software to be built, which will reduce the uncertainties. The actual performance will also need to be monitored against the plans, so that corrective action can be taken as the need arises.

What is done at these stages depends upon the nature of the software that is being developed, and how the various problems associated with software development will be solved. These problems arise from the sheer size and complexity of the systems, and because the systems are being built by human beings for other human beings.

A system must meet the needs of the customer and the customer's organization. These needs must be identified. This can be done by working with the customer and users at the start of the analysis phase identified above. The list of requirements need not be completed at this phase. Indeed, an understanding of the organization's needs will evolve as the software is developed, with 'changes' happening throughout the process. Some approaches to software development are based on building a series of prototypes that evolve into the final product using feedback from customers and users throughout the software development process. The main objective is to ensure that the development process results in a system that satisfies the customer. These processes of checking with the customer are called **validation** and may involve formal review meetings, prototype demonstrations, or even informal contact. Thus, validation is the process of checking that the software does what the customer wants.

Once the needs are understood, at least in part, the implementation of the system can start. This may proceed in many ways. But each of these ways will always involve elements of specification, design, implementation (coding) and testing. **Requirements specification** requires the developer to record in precise terms what it is that should be implemented. **Design** involves deciding how to achieve this requirements specification technically as opposed to managerially. **Programming** (or **coding**) involves coding the system, which is only a very small part of the overall process. **Testing** the system requires the developer to ensure that it works technically and that it meets its objectives and specification. Each part of the system being developed will involve the sequence of specification, design, coding and testing, but one or more of these parts may also be developed in parallel. During these processes the developer constantly checks that the design corresponds to the specification, that the programming is correctly coded and that the specification and design are tested correctly. These cross-checks are known as **verification**, and may address not just functional correctness, but also important features such as performance.

Carrying out a comprehensive engineering process with validation and verification reviews, managed with appropriate project management methods, is important for ensuring the quality of the final software product. However, under the normal pressures of developing the software to schedule and budget, some project managers and their software engineers may be tempted to cut corners. It is common to have an independent **quality assurance** process also working as guardians of the system's quality, thus ensuring that the intended good engineering practice is indeed followed.

1 Access the course web page for *Unit 1.1* and read Articles 1–5 in *The 'Killer Robot' Case*, where you will be introduced to the importance of management and quality issues in software development.

Distribution means concurrent systems

Distributed systems are by far the most common kind of software system being built today. The majority of businesses are distributed and the software supports these businesses. A **distributed system** is one in which the separate parts of the system execute on different computers and communicate with one another to achieve their purpose. In more abstract terms, this means that a distributed software application consists of a number of programs executing simultaneously and exchanging data on an unpredictable basis. Such systems are said to be **concurrent**. As soon as you begin to examine concurrent systems in detail, a whole new range of issues arise. Some applications are inherently concurrent and consist of a number of separate activities that have to be managed if they are to work successfully together.

Managing concurrently executing programs raises many complex issues. In general, these executing programs, or processes as they are called, will interact with other processes. Interacting processes can execute either on the same processor or on different processors. This means that processes have to synchronize their actions. For example, if one process wants to send data to another process it must do so in such a way that the second process can accept the data. It is no use if the sender outputs the data when the receiver is not in a position to read the data. One solution to this problem is to make the sending process wait (*block* and *suspend* are alternative terms) until the receiver is ready.

Processes will also make use of resources (such as data, files and printers) and situations will arise where processes will compete for resources. If two processes are competing for the same resource, some mechanism will have to be found to prioritize between them. A severe case of competition occurs when two processes are each currently using resources required by the other; neither can proceed. This is a situation known as **deadlock**. These are just some of the issues that arise in concurrent systems. Distributed systems are inherently concurrent and involve the extra dimension of networking. Therefore, we have devoted a considerable portion of the course to examining this area. Without knowing the issues relating to concurrent systems, it is impossible to design good quality distributed systems.

The excitement surrounding the programming language, Java, comes from its use as a language for writing programs designed for networking, specifically the Internet. It is a language that has good support for writing concurrent systems and will be studied in detail throughout Block 1.

2 If you are interested, read Budd, Section 2.1 and the introduction to Section 2.2, where you will find a more detailed discussion of Java and client-server systems.

Security is an essential quality of distributed systems

Security is a word that describes a wide spectrum of extremely important issues in distributed systems. As soon as two computers communicate (that is, exchange data) a number of very significant problems arise. First, the data could be a program which, when executed on the recipient machine, causes untold chaos, either maliciously, in the case of a virus, or accidentally in the case of a poorly designed program. Second, the transmission of data must be secure, that is, it must be received unchanged. Third, the data must not have been intercepted during its transmission (think of the damage that could be done by an eavesdropper learning about your credit card details). The design of networks, the kinds of data permitted to be transmitted, and encryption techniques all play a part in ensuring security.

Other important aspects of security are preventing unauthorized access to data and authenticating users of the system.

> 3 If you are interested, read Budd, Subsection 2.2.2, where you will see the role that Java plays in the area of security.

Human–computer interaction (HCI)

It is important that any software system must be usable by those who have to interact with it. A good design will separate out the business functions from those that support **human–computer interaction** (that part of the software that interacts directly with the human). The **usability** of a software system means the ease with which a human can interact with the software. A poor design, from the point of view of human–computer interaction, will make it very difficult for the business to take advantage of the functionality of the software. Many systems have been functionally correct, but failed in operation because they failed to satisfy simple usability criteria.

The environment in which a software system is used plays a significant role in the design of human–computer interaction. What might be considered good design in one environment may be totally inappropriate in another.

> 4 If you are interested, access the course web page for *Unit 1.1* and read Article 6 in *The 'Killer Robot' Case*, where you will see the significance of HCI in software development.

Software tools

In this course you will be introduced to two software tools:

- an integrated development environment (IDE) for Java;
- a tool for constructing models using the Unified Modelling Language (UML).

They are examples of computer-aided software engineering (CASE) tools. In any large project, such software tools can help manage complexity. The two tools we have provided with this course will illustrate the kinds of support that software tools can provide.

The IDE will enable you to construct Java programs as a managed collection of source files. It will enable you to test programs and remove errors within a controlled environment. The IDE contains a compiler (for detecting errors and translating Java source code into bytecode for subsequent execution) and a debugger (for investigating how an executing program behaves).

A modelling tool is used throughout the software development process and is used to produce diagrams that describe various aspects of the system. In this course you will see that there are various categories of model that describe different stages of the development process. Eventually, a model will be implemented in a programming language to form the application. Many such modelling tools are very sophisticated and provide support for team working and reverse engineering, that is, taking an existing program and producing a model.

The case study

To make the above ideas more concrete, a substantial case study has been provided as part of the course materials. The case study will examine all aspects of the development of a software system so that you can gain a better understanding of the process in context. Without a context it will be difficult to appreciate the reasons why certain decisions are taken and to understand why good software development is as much about understanding a business, having good project management and recognizing the need to keep quality issues to the fore, as having an armoury of tools and techniques for writing programs.

The aim of this first reading from the case study is to appreciate the scale and complexity of a typical software problem. While the initial description of a problem, often called the statement of requirements, may be quite brief and, at first sight, apparently simple, the factors that a software engineer must take into account from the outset can be quite extensive.

The Case Study can be accessed from the M301 Web site (http://M301.open.ac.uk).

5 Read the first section of the *Case Study* entitled *The Case Study background,* which deals with user requirements.

6 Do the SAQs and exercises in the *Case Study* relevant to that section.

1.4 SAQ and solution

SAQ 1.1

(a) What are the two main elements of software maintenance?

(b) What are the roles of a specification?

(c) What two tasks can be identified during the analysis phase of a software development?

(d) Distinguish between validation and verification.

(e) What is a distributed system?

(f) What is meant by saying that processes are synchronized?

(g) What are the three aspects of security that affect distributed systems?

Solution

(a) Correcting faults and enhancement.

(b) A specification can be the basis of a contract between a customer and a developer. It defines what the customer wants and tells the developer what to produce. Note that some developments can use continuous evolution having users as part of the team and consequently they do not have a specification.

(c) Requirements elicitation and requirements specification.

(d) **Validation** is the process of ensuring that the specification meets the customer's needs. **Verification** is the process of ensuring that the product is built to its specification.

(e) A **distributed system** is one in which the separate parts of the system execute on different computers and these parts must communicate with one another to achieve their purpose.

(f) The actions of the processes must be coordinated so that, for example, one process is in a state to receive a message when another process wishes to send that message.

(g) Security means: (i) preventing the execution of a program that could cause untold chaos, (ii) transmitting data in such a way that it is received unchanged, (iii) preventing data from being intercepted during transmission and (iv) authentication of users.

1.5 Exercise and solution

Exercise 1.1

From your reading of the first article of *The 'Killer Robot' Case* answer the following question. The article accuses the programmer of negligence, but can you say which aspects of the software development process (as discussed in the course so far) were allegedly not carried out properly?

Solution

The article contains very little hard evidence of what actually happened, but it is clear that the implementation (the program) did not match the specification (the formulae for the equations of motion). The programmer is accused of negligently misinterpreting the specification, which is another way of saying that there was a lapse in verification. However, it can be argued that the specification itself was inadequate ('scrawled on a piece of paper') and that it was ambiguous and therefore open to misinterpretation. One inference is that no validation (checking back with the customer) took place. There is no mention in the article about reviews or of testing, or indeed of any quality assurance procedures which might have revealed the inadequacies of both the specification and the implementation. Whatever else may have been wrong with the process, it seems equally clear that neither the person who provided the specification nor the programmer acted in an acceptably professional way.

1.6 Summary of section

In this section you have been introduced to the main themes of the course and have examined the statement of requirements of a case study to which reference will be made throughout the course. You have also been introduced to the human side of software development in which project management, human–computer interaction and ethical considerations are paramount. In so doing, you have met some of the terminology that will pervade the course.

2 INTRODUCTION TO THE INTEGRATED DEVELOPMENT ENVIRONMENT (IDE)

In this section you will learn the rudimentary facilities of one of the main tools used in the course: the integrated development environment or IDE. An IDE is a software tool that enables you to develop applications. It will be used throughout the course.

2.1 Objectives

On completion of this section you should be able to:

1 set up a directory suitable for your practical work in Java;

2 create a new *project* using the IDE;

3 create a Java *source file* containing a small class;

4 compile and execute a Java application;

5 use the help facility in the IDE.

2.2 Key terms and concepts

The important terms and concepts associated with this section are as follows.

application	execute	import (source code)
browser	Help facility	project
compile	IDE	source file
component		

2.3 Learning to use the IDE

In this section you will start learning how to use the integrated development environment (IDE), which is provided as part of the course materials. In Section 3 and in later units of this block you will continue to study the facilities it offers. The IDE will be used throughout the course for developing Java programs. While the purpose of this section is to learn about the IDE, you will also be introduced to some of the Java programs on which the first block of the course is based. It is not the intention of this section to teach you how to program in Java but it should help you to become familiar with the layout and composition of typical Java programs.

The work of this section is entirely practical and you will need to use your computer. It is important that you do the following activity as you will not be able to do later practical work if you do not.

> Work through all the Practical Activities in Sections 1 and 2 of the *IDE Handbook*. When you have completed this work, attempt the SAQ in Subsection 2.4.

2.4 SAQ and solution

SAQ 2.1

(a) What is a Java source file?

(b) What does a project (a .jpr file) consist of?

(c) How many source code files can there be in a project?

Solution

(a) A Java source file is a text file containing some Java code (typically it contains the definition of a class).

(b) A project contains the following information: a list of Java source files, a list of directories in which to look for source files, a directory name for where the project's class files are put and the name of the file that contains the main class.

(c) There is no restriction on the number of source code files in a project. However, a project should contain all the source code files required for an application if that application is to be comprehensible and maintainable.

2.5 Summary of section

In this section you have learned how to set up an appropriate directory structure for your Java work, and how to use an IDE for constructing Java programs (applications). In particular, you have seen that a Java program consists of a collection of classes and that each class is contained within a separate text file. A project contains the information necessary for development, compilation and running. A Java project must be successfully compiled (translated into bytecode) before the program can be executed. The compilation process checks for errors in the source code. You have also learned how to use the Help facility in the IDE.

3 FIRST PROGRAM IN JAVA

In this section you will learn about the Java constructs used in the first class you created when learning about the IDE in Section 2. It should take you an evening to work through this section but we have allowed an extra evening for the unit as a whole because we appreciate that it will take time for you to become familiar with the course materials and the style of the course.

An important note

It is *not* our intention that you should develop a high level of skill in Java programming in this course. In the early units we expect you to gain a reading knowledge of Java and be able to make small, straight-forward changes to relatively small programs. You should not expect to understand fully every aspect of the early programs the first time you meet them; your understanding of Java programming will develop as the course progresses. We *do* expect that you will become sufficiently familiar with Java constructs so that you will be able to describe how programs that are designed for networking purposes function.

We anticipate that the majority of students will have studied M206, *Computing: An Object-oriented Approach* prior to studying M301. This means that you are likely to have a good understanding of the language Smalltalk (those of you who have not had this experience can now move directly to Subsection 3.1 if you wish, but you may find that you can pick up some useful points in the next paragraph).

One of the purposes of M301 is to introduce you to an alternative to Smalltalk, particularly to a language that exhibits something known as *strong typing*. Such languages, of which Java is an example, enable certain sorts of errors to be detected before a program is executed, a characteristic that supports programming discipline and reliability of systems. This means that you will have to adjust to a different kind of programming style, which should not be a problem for those who have already been exposed to a strongly typed language. Therefore, to help Smalltalk programmers to bridge the gap more easily, we have provided an appendix to this unit which directly addresses the similarities and differences between Smalltalk and Java. You might like to read the appendix now *before* continuing your study with Subsection 3.1.

3.1 Objectives

On completion of this section you should be able to:

1. understand some of the basic Java constructs needed to create a simple executable Java program, which includes the structure of a program, a class, a method, a data field, and the use of modifiers;
2. describe the role of the `main` method when a Java program is executed;
3. describe the model of execution of a Java program including the roles of variables and method invocation (or message passing);
4. understand the need for, and how to write, declarations;
5. understand the difference between types, abstract data types and classes.

3.2 Key terms and concepts

The important terms and concepts associated with this section are as follows.

abstract data type	dot notation	object
access modifier	implementational view	packages
application	**import** (package)	primitive data types
assignment	instance	**private**
class	lifetime modifier	**protected**
class body	**main** method	**public**
class header	member	return type
command-line argument	message passing	**static**
conceptual view	method	type
data field	modifier	**void**

3.3 Study activities

Before attempting this section you should have completed Subsection 2.3 where you would have created and executed the Java program named FirstProjectClass (in this section of work, your task is to gain an understanding of the programming constructs used in that program).

Terms specific to Java are shown in our bold Java font, for example, **import**.

Your main task in this section is to read Budd, Chapter 4, but before you do this it would be useful for you to have an understanding of the following ideas about the model of computation used in Java. Since there are a number of possibly new ideas here, we do not want you to spend a great deal of time at this stage trying to come to grips with all the detail. Instead we suggest that you read through the discussion quickly and return to it once you have read Budd, Chapter 4. Thereafter, use this subsection as reference material. The ideas are:

1 the nature of the relationship between *objects*, *classes* and *method invocation* (or *message sending*);

2 the difference between *classes* and *primitive data types* in Java;

3 the connection between *variables* and *declarations* in Java;

4 the use of the terms, *type*, *abstract data type*, *class*, *value* and *object*;

5 how data is input to and output from Java *methods*.

Objects, classes and calling methods in Java

Budd, Figure 4.3 shows a simple example of a Java class named BankAccount, which is repeated here for convenience.

```
class BankAccount {
  private int accountBalance = 0;
  public void deposit (int amount) {
     accountBalance = accountBalance + amount;
  }
  public void withdrawal (int amount) {
     accountBalance = accountBalance - amount;
  }
}
```

In Java terminology, this class contains three **members** named accountBalance, deposit and withdrawal. The first member, accountBalance, is a **data field** initialized to zero; more precisely it is an instance field because it references an instance of a class (i.e. an object) or holds a primitive type. It is sometimes called an **instance variable**, as in Smalltalk. The other two members, deposit and withdrawal, are **methods**.

In another class you could create a BankAccount object and call/invoke methods on it. In the object-oriented paradigm we often describe this as sending messages to the object. What this means is that a method, a piece of program that performs some computation, is executed in response to the message.

For example, you could declare a variable, say myAccount, and make it refer to a new BankAccount object:

```
BankAccount myAccount = new BankAccount ();
```

Notice that = in Java acts in the same way as := in Smalltalk. The details of precisely what this statement means will be given in a later unit. For now, all you need to know is that the result of carrying out this statement is shown in Figure 3.1.

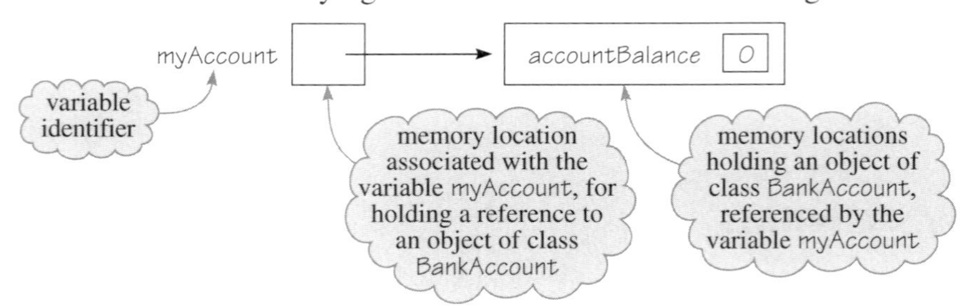

Figure 3.1 A variable refers to an object

The actual object referred to by myAccount contains a single data field — an integer variable named accountBalance. Since every instance of the class BankAccount will have such a data field, it is known as an instance variable. When an object of class BankAccount is created, its instance variable (data field) will be initialized to zero, as defined in its declaration:

```
private int accountBalance = 0;
```

Once the object referenced by myAccount has been created, messages can be sent to it. For example, to add 100 to the accountBalance of the object referred to by myAccount, you would write:

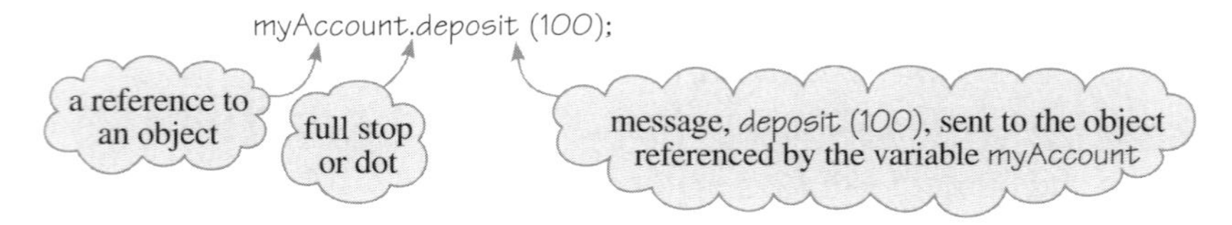

Figure 3.2 The dot notation used in message passing (method calls)

In Java, it is more usual to say that a method is *called* or *invoked* on an object, rather than saying a *message is sent* to an object. In this course, we will follow the Java convention.

Note the full stop between the variable identifier, myAccount, and the name of the method, deposit. This is an example of what is commonly known as the **dot notation** used in many OO languages to denote sending a message (in this case, deposit (100)) to an object (here, referenced by myAccount). We also say that, when a message is sent to an object, the consequence is that the method referred to in the message is executed (or invoked or called).

Note *Full stops are used in various places within a Java program with different meanings. A full stop does not always signify invoking (calling) a method, but its meaning should be obvious from the context.*

Rather than continually using the rather long phrase 'the object referred to by the variable myAccount' we often contract it to 'the object myAccount'.

Here is a sequence of method invocations on the object myAccount which will perform a series of deposits and withdrawals from the bank account that will leave myAccount with a balance of 44:

```
myAccount.deposit (100);
myAccount.withdrawal (30);
myAccount.withdrawal (26);
```

In Java, each of the lines above would be described as a **statement**, and a Java method would consist of a sequence of statements, each one terminated with a semicolon. myAccount is known as a variable because the object to which it refers can change as the program is executed. For example, suppose that there were two BankAccount objects, referred to by the variables myAccount and yourAccount. The following statement, an example of an assignment statement,

```
yourAccount = myAccount;
```

would result in the variable yourAccount referring to the same object as myAccount as illustrated in Figure 3.3. That is, the reference of myAccount has been copied into yourAccount.

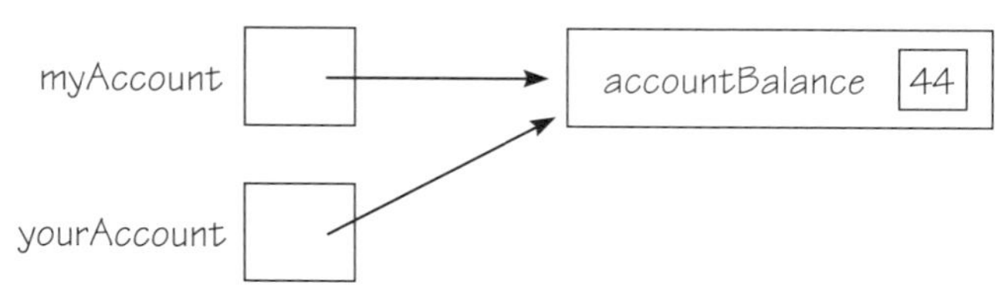

Figure 3.3 Two variables reference the same object

Figure 3.3 shows that the two variables refer to the same object (represented by the large rectangle). In this particular example, the object contains one data field (accountBalance). The variables do not reference the value of this data field directly.

The result of executing this assignment is that subsequent messages sent to either myAccount or yourAccount will be sent to the same object. This implies that the object would be updated in exactly the same way by either

```
myAccount.deposit (50);
```

or

```
yourAccount.deposit (50);
```

until such times that either myAccount or yourAccount is made to refer to another object.

Having two (or more) variables reference the same object is known as aliasing and must be used with care.

Primitive data types and classes in Java

Java distinguishes between primitive data types and classes. Primitive data types include: int (short for integer), float (often referred to as 'real' in other languages), double (double precision real), boolean, and char (short for character). Primitive data types are part of the language definition in which int is the name of a primitive data type consisting of the set of integers in the range –2 147 483 648 to 2 147 483 647 inclusive; boolean is the set of values consisting of true and false; and char represents the ISO Unicode character set.

There are, in fact, four kinds of integer types: byte, short, int and long, which represent different ranges of integer values and occupy different amounts of storage.

Classes are program constructs containing methods and data fields whose definitions can be inspected by the programmer. New classes can be defined from existing classes through the mechanisms of inheritance and interfacing (which will be examined in a later unit).

There are several reasons why primitive data types are distinguished from classes, the main one being efficiency and this manifests itself in the mechanisms used for variables in the two cases.

In the case of objects, variables are used to refer to objects as illustrated in Figure 3.1. Java does not use the reference mechanism for variables of primitive data type. Instead, the values are stored in the variable itself. Figure 3.4 shows an example.

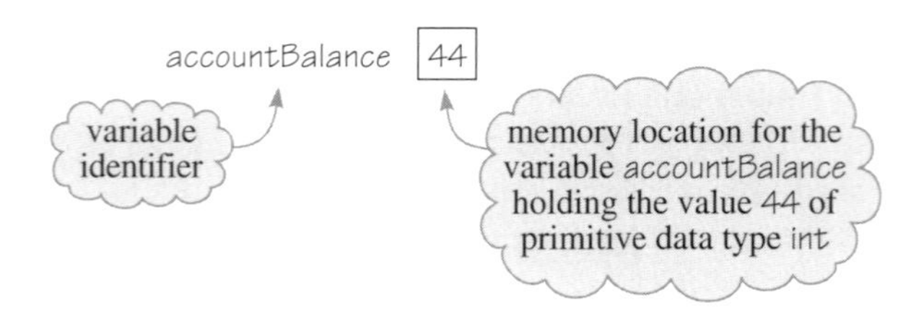

Figure 3.4 The physical representation of a variable of primitive data type int

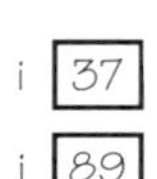

Figure 3.5 Two variables of primitive data type int

Figure 3.6 Two variables of primitive data type with the same value

This difference between the physical representation of values of the primitive data types and that of objects is significant, particularly in the area of assignment. For example, suppose that there were two variables of primitive data type int, as shown in Figure 3.5.

The assignment,

```
i = j;
```

is shown in Figure 3.6.

The assignment *copies* the value of j into the variable i. The result is that both i and j have the value 89, but they are totally independent. Any subsequent change to the value of i, for example, does not affect the value of j. Compare this situation with that shown in Figure 3.3 where two variables refer to the same object, and note the comments that immediately follow Figure 3.3.

Variables and declarations

An important feature of Java (in common with many OO languages) is that a variable may only refer to objects of a specific class or a specific primitive data type (this is called the **type** of the variable). This restriction is useful because it enables checks to be made for certain kinds of programming error. This means that every variable must be *declared* as having a particular type. That is, every variable must appear in a *declaration* in which the class of the objects to which it may refer or the primitive data type of the values it contains must be stated explicitly. Here are some examples of Java declarations you have met so far:

```
private int accountBalance = 0;
BankAccount myAccount = new BankAccount ();
String [ ] args;
int amount;
```

These declarations denote that the variable

- accountBalance (and amount) is of type int (because it is declared with primitive data type int);
- myAccount is of type BankAccount (because it is declared with the class BankAccount);
- args is of type array (because it is declared with [ ]);

A declaration can begin with one or more modifiers (which are keywords such as **private** in the first example).

Modifiers will be dealt with in detail later.

After the modifiers, if any, comes the name of a class (or primitive data type in the case of int in the last example) followed by the name of the variable. In the first two examples, the variables have also been specifically initialized (accountBalance to zero and myAccount to refer to a new BankAccount object). In the last two examples, args will be allowed to refer to an array of String objects and amount will represent an integer value.

Types, abstract data types and classes in M301

You will find that the terms *type*, *abstract data type* and *class* occur throughout the literature on software development and programming languages with varying meanings. For the purposes of consistency in M301 we have chosen certain definitions for these terms which we shall now discuss. But before doing so, we need to draw your attention to the difference between

> thinking about how to solve a problem that involves understanding the problem (or application) domain which has nothing to do with programming languages, a process that leads to what we describe as the conceptual view of the solution,

and

> implementing the solution to a problem in a particular programming language that requires a knowledge of the syntax and semantics of that language, a process that leads to what we describe as the **implementational view** of the solution.

When analysing a problem it is possible to identify collections of items in the problem domain with similar properties, for example, employees in a firm, for which it is useful to invent a collective name, such as 'employees'. It is then possible to discuss the type 'employee' which is the set of employees in the firm. This implies that certain items have the property of being an employee whereas other items are not employees (some items are in the set, others are not). Thus we end up with the following definition of 'type'.

Type is a word given to a named set of items having some property in common.

It turns out that a useful way of defining the property, which the elements of a set have in common, is to list the operations in which they can participate and to use the term **behaviour** to stand for this collection of operations. This leads us to the idea of an abstract data type.

An **abstract data type (ADT)** is a set of items defined by the collection of operations that can be carried out on them. The elements of such a set are usually referred to as **values**.

An example of an ADT is a set of bank accounts. Let us call such a set `Account`. Being an ADT, all the instances of `Account` (i.e. all the individual bank accounts that make up the set) will respond to the same operations (i.e. exhibit the same behaviour). So, for example, the balance of an account might be set using the operation `setBalance`, the existing balance obtained using `getBalance`, money withdrawn from the account using `withdrawAmount`, money transferred from the account to another account using `transferAmount`, and so on. In other words, all the instances of `Account` are characterized by the same collection of operations — any objects that respond to the same collection of operations would be considered to be bank accounts. This raises the question of what is meant by the same collection of operations. It is not possible at this point to analyse what it means for one operation to be the same as another. Suffice to say that, to be considered the same, operations must have the same syntax and the same semantics (i.e. informally, they must have the same heading and they must do the same thing).

This brings us to the idea of a class. The word 'class' has several meanings and there are three we are interested in:

- a **class** is an implementation of an abstract data type;
- a **class** is a programming structure containing a collection of data fields and methods;
- a **class** is a set of objects.

Thus, a class is a collection of objects and the objects are defined by a set of methods that correspond to the operations of the ADT. These methods will, in general, be implemented in terms of data fields and other methods contained within the class. The methods that implement the operations will be *public* (and therefore available for use in other classes) whereas the other methods and data fields will be *private* (available for use only within the class).

Therefore, we can now speak of 'the type of an object', by which is meant the name of the abstract data type defined by the public methods of a class, and 'the class of an object', synonymously.

Note that each argument of a method also has a type (it is defined in the heading of the method). Strong typing means that the actual argument, which appears in a message, must be of the same type (or subclass of this type) as defined in the method heading.

The significance of all this is revealed when we examine the idea of *strong typing*. Most object-oriented languages use variables to refer to values of primitive data types and objects. In a strongly typed language, a type (class) is associated with every variable via a declaration. In a strongly typed language, such as Java, a given variable is allowed only to refer to an object or value of its declared type (or, as you will see when dealing with inheritance, a variable may refer to an object of a subclass of the variable's declared type). This implies that only those operations (methods) defining the type of the variable may be applied to the objects or values to which the variable refers.

This discussion now enables us to understand phrases such as 'the type of a variable', 'the type of an argument' and 'the return type of a function' in which the word 'type' stands for either the name of a primitive data type or the name of a class.

Methods

As you will see in detail when you read Budd, Chapter 4 a *method* in Java is composed of two parts: a *heading* and a *body* . The heading consists of four elements:

1 its name;
2 the names and types of its arguments;
3 the type of the object or primitive data type it returns as output (if any);
4 the modifier(s) (access and/or lifetime).

Arguments are also known as **parameters**. In fact, the usual convention is to favour parameters. See below.

These elements are illustrated in Figure 3.7 where the headings of two different methods (from different classes) are given. (The definition of a method always starts with a heading.)

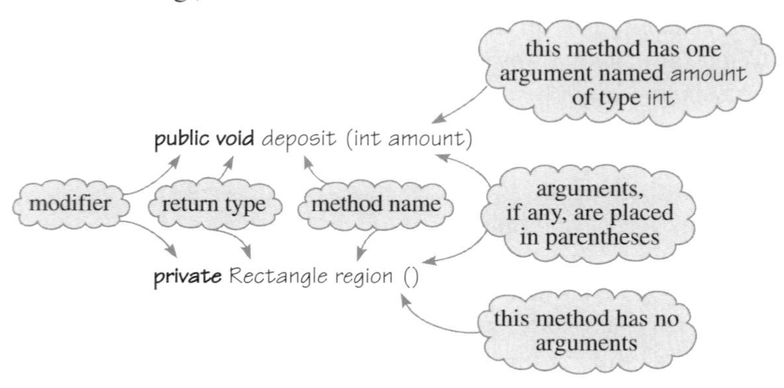

Figure 3.7 Headings of methods

In general, a method is a small part of a program that is supplied with some objects (or values of primitive data type) called **arguments** , and whose purpose is to perform a computation, possibly producing an object (or a value of a primitive data type) as its result.

A modifier, if any, is always the first item in a method heading. There can be more than one modifier. The second item is the name of the class or primitive data type of the result (for example, Rectangle and **void** in Figure 3.7). The keyword **void** is used to signify that a method does not return a result.

The third item in the heading is the name of the method, and finally there is a list of zero, one or more arguments enclosed in parentheses (the parentheses always appear, even if there are no arguments). Each argument is described by the name of either a class or primitive data type followed by the name of the argument.

From a method's heading, the format (or syntax) of a message can be deduced. The message causes the method's body to be executed (or invoked, or called). For example, here are typical uses of the methods in Figure 3.7:

```
myAccount.deposit (100);
myBall.region ();
```

where myAccount and myBall are sent the messages *deposit (100)* and *region ()* respectively. In the message *deposit (100)*, the value 100 is known as an **actual argument** which, when the method *deposit* is invoked, is assigned to the **formal argument**, *amount*, appearing in the method heading. During the execution of the body of *deposit*, the formal argument *amount* acts as a local variable.

The above examples show that the form of a message is based on two elements of a method heading: its name, and its formal arguments. A particular message will, of course, provide actual arguments in place of the formal arguments.

Some authors insist that in Java the term **parameter** is exclusively used for formal arguments, and the term **argument** is used for actual arguments. However, in this course we will use the terms interchangeably.

A method **signature** defines everything you need to know about a method to call it, i.e. its modifiers, return type, name, and parameters. In Java, methods whose signatures differ only in their return types are not allowed.

1. Read Budd, Chapter 4 (ignore the second paragraph in section 4.1 and its associated Figure 4.2 since they deal with an operating system, Unix, with which you may be unfamiliar.) Remember to read the explanatory notes, if any, associated with each section.
2. At the end of each section of Budd, Chapter 4, attempt the relevant SAQ (it is labelled with the same number as the section).
3. Read the second section of the *Case Study* entitled *Implementing a collection*, which contains examples of the use of arrays, **if** statements and **for** loops. There is no need to study this section in detail at this stage: use it as a source of further examples of the Java constructs introduced in this unit.
4. Finally, when you have completed the above, attempt the exercises in Subsection 3.5 and check whether any further exercises from Budd, Chapter 4 are included in the TMA for this unit.

Explanatory notes

1 The execution of Java programs (Budd, Section 4.1)

Towards the end of Section 4.1, Budd uses the phrase 'initial method for execution' when describing the method main. The meaning of this phrase can be understood as follows. A Java program consists of a collection of classes each of which contains definitions of data fields and methods. In order to begin the execution of the program, the Java interpreter has to be told where to start. Java, in common with some other languages, always begins execution with the statements contained in a method called main. If you do not supply a method named main and declare it to be both **public** and **static**, the Java interpreter will not know where to start.

It is possible to construct a program containing several classes each having a main method in which case you will have to state which of the main methods is used to start the program. Having identified the main method, execution proceeds with the execution of the statements within the body of main. Typically, these statements will create new objects and send messages to them.

2 Arrays in Java (Budd, Section 4.3)

In Java, an array is an ordered list of elements of the same class (or primitive data type). Each element of an array is associated with an integer index representing a specific numbered position in the array such that the first value in the array is always associated with index 0. For example, Figure 3.8 shows an array called name, whose elements are of type String, containing the names of six people.

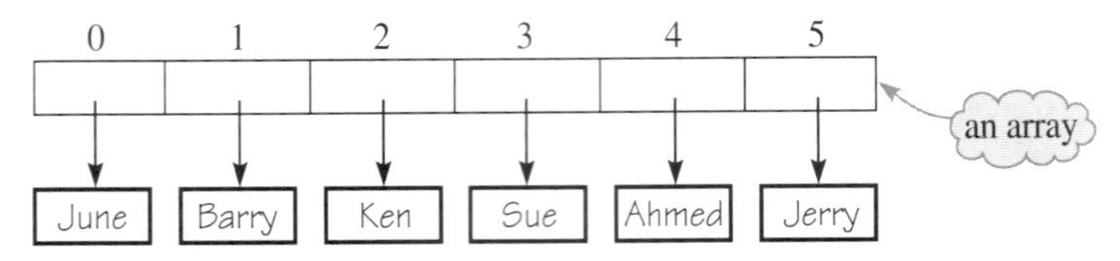

Figure 3.8 An array of strings

Thus, the first value in the array, denoted by name [0], refers to the string June. The third value of the array is denoted name [2] and refers to the string Ken. To access an element of an array, you use the name of the array followed by the index in square brackets. To place a value into an array at a specific index you use an assignment statement such as:

```
name [4] = "Ali"
```

which places the string Ali at index position 4 in the array name, replacing the element (Ahmed) that was there previously.

The elements of a given array are either references to objects (from the same class, such as String in the above example) or values of the same primitive data type.

An array has a fixed number of elements *which must be specified when the array is created* (you will see how this is done in *Unit 1.2*). However, the number of items is not specified when an array *variable* is declared (as a data field or a formal argument of a method).

3 The syntax of an if statement (Budd, Section 4.3)

An **if** statement allows you to choose between alternative courses of action depending upon the value of a boolean expression. The syntax of an **if** statement is:

```
if ( boolean expression ) {
  sequence-of-statements
}
else {
  sequence-of-statements
}
```

If either sequence-of-statements contains only one statement, the curly braces surrounding the single statement can be omitted, but it is good practice to keep them in.

The boolean expression must be placed in parentheses: if its value is true, the first sequence of statements enclosed in braces is executed; if its value is false, the second sequence of statements following the keyword **else** and enclosed in braces is executed. The **else** part of the **if** statement, that is, everything following (and including) the **else** keyword, is optional. If it is omitted and the boolean expression is false, the **if** statement performs no actions and the execution of the program continues with the next statement following it.

4 The dot notation used with data fields (Budd, Section 4.3)

In the class SecondProgram, the construction args.length occurs and the text says that length is a data field. Here, the dot notation is being used to denote a data field named length that occurs in the class String (because the type of the argument args is String).

We know that length must be a data field because it does not have parentheses following the name as would be the case if it were a method.

3.4 SAQs and solutions

'Study Questions' are from Budd, Chapter 4.

SAQ 4.1

(a) What is the original meaning of the word *paradigm*? (Study Question 1)
(b) What is the overall structure of a Java program? (Study Question 2)
(c) What are the two components of a class description? (Study Question 3)
(d) How is the body of a class delineated? (Study Question 4)
(e) What are the two types of members that can be found in a class body? (Study Question 5)
(f) What is the connection between a class name and the file it is stored in? (Study Question 6)
(g) What is a method? (Study Question 7)
(h) What are the parts of a method header? (Study Question 8)
(i) What does a class consist of?
(j) How is the body of a method delineated?
(k) What does a method body comprise?

Solution

(a) A paradigm is an example sentence that can be used as a model in learning a language.
(b) The overall structure of a Java program is a collection of class descriptions.
(c) The two major parts of a class description are the class header and the class body.
(d) The body of a class is contained within curly braces.
(e) The two types of members that can be found in a class body are data field and method.
(f) They must both have the same name.
(g) A method defines the code (a set of operations) that is executed when that method is invoked on an object.
(h) A method header can have modifiers (optional), a return type, a name, and argument(s), if any, enclosed in parentheses.
(i) A class consists of a collection of members.
(j) The body of a method is contained within braces, { and }.
(k) A method body is a sequence of statements.

SAQ 4.2

(a) What operation is performed by `System.out.println`? (Study Question 9)
(b) What is the purpose of an `import` statement? (Study Question 10)
(c) In `System.out.println ("Your first Java program!")`, what is `out`?

Solution

(a) It prints out a string value on the computer's screen.
(b) An `import` statement makes a portion of the Java library visible to the following class description.
(c) It is a data field (class variable) of the class System. It cannot be a method, otherwise it would have been written with parentheses, out ().

SAQ 4.3

(a) What is the type void mainly used for? (Study Question 11)

(b) What does the difference in case in the initial letter of the types int and String indicate? (Study Question 12)

(c) How in Java does one determine the number of elements held in an array? (Study Question 13)

(d) What kind of values are of type float and double?

Solution

(a) The type **void** is used to show that a method does not return a value. Such a method is also known as a *procedure*.

(b) There is a convention that names of classes begin with an upper-case letter. String is the name of a class. There is no class named int in Java: int is the name of a primitive data type.

(c) The number of elements held in an array can be found by means of a special property associated with every array named length. Thus, if arg is the name of an array, the number of elements currently in arg can be found by sending it the message length as in arg.length.

(d) The primitive data types float and double describe floating-point values, that is, numerical values having a decimal part (e.g. 3.1415). The difference between float and double is in the amount of storage space allocated to values of each type. More space is allocated to values of type double so that they can contain more decimal digits than float values can thereby making values of type double more precise than values of type float. The term double is meant to convey the idea that it represents decimal values with twice the precision of float values (although this may not be exactly the case, we often speak of 'double precision').

SAQ 4.4

(a) What is the meaning of the + operator when one of the arguments is a String? (Study Question 14)

(b) What are the three access modifier keywords? (Study Question 15)

(c) To what can access modifiers be applied?

(d) What is wrong with the following?

```
private static void main (String [ ] args) { ... }
```

Solution

(a) The operator +, when one of its arguments is of type String, converts the non-String argument into a string and concatenates ('adds') the second argument on to the end of the first argument.

(b) The three access modifier keywords and their purposes are:

- **public** — the data field, method or class to which it is applied is visible to, i.e. available to be used by, all objects of all other classes in addition to the class in which it is defined;
- **private** — the data field, or method to which it is applied is not visible to objects of classes outside the class in which it is defined, including subclasses;
- **protected** — the data field, or method to which it is applied is visible only to those objects outside the class in which it is defined that are heirs, i.e. subclasses, of that class. It makes sense to allow subclasses to access the private members of its parent class even though client classes cannot do so. A protected member is also visible to all classes in its package (if it has been defined as part of one).

Java packages provide a mechanism for grouping together related classes. In our view, a bad feature of Java is that it allows client classes access to protected data fields in the server class. It means that such client classes may access protected data fields and hence circumvent interface methods that have been designed to access such data fields.

(c) Access modifiers can be applied to data fields and methods. The modifier **public** can also be applied to a class.

(d) The main method must be declared public, otherwise it would be hidden from the system and therefore the execution of the program would not start.

SAQ 4.5

When applied to a data member, what does the modifier static signify? (Study Question 16)

Solution

When applied to a data field, **static** signifies that the data field is shared by all the objects of the class. A static variable is also known as a class variable to distinguish it from a non-static variable known as an instance variable because each object has its own copy of the instance variable.

Note that a static member, be it a method or a data field, exists even if no objects of its class have been created. Consequently, like the method main, which is always declared static, all static members are available for use when a program starts executing, and before any objects have been created.

3.5 Exercises and solutions

[Remember to check whether an exercise from Budd, Chapter 4 is required for this year's TMA.]

Exercise 3.1 (Budd, Chapter 4 Exercise 1)

Add a member method named display to the following class description.

```
public class BankAccount {
   private int accountBalance = 0;

   public void deposit (int amount) {
      accountBalance = accountBalance + amount;
   }
   public void withdrawal (int amount) {
      accountBalance = accountBalance - amount;
   }
}
```

Solution

The method display can be defined as follows.

```
public void display () {
   System.out.println (accountBalance);
}
```

Exercise 3.2 (Budd, Chapter 4 Exercise 2)

The looping statement in Java uses the for keyword, and consists of three parts. The first part is an initialization statement, which can also be used to declare the loop variable. The second part is a test for termination; the loop will execute as long as the expression remains true. The final part is the increment, which is a statement that is evaluated to update the loop variable.

A *command-line argument* is an argument provided by a user to a running program. We will see later how to provide these arguments in the IDE, by way of a properties window. The name refers to operating systems in which programs are controlled by typing into a strictly sequential interface. The latest line, the line on which you would be typing, is referred to as the *command line*. For us, the command line arguments are the elements of args.

Consider the following main program. Describe the effect produced by the program when it is executed with three command-line arguments.

```
public static void main ( String [ ] args ) {
  for (int i = 0; i < args.length; i = i + 1)
   System.out.println(args [i]);
}
```

Solution

Since there are three command-line arguments, the array args will have three elements. Hence, the value returned by args.length will be 3. The loop variable, i, starts at 0 (int i = 0), is incremented by 1 each time the loop body is completed, and the looping finishes once i is greater than or equal to 3 (i.e. looping continues while i < 3). The body of the loop displays on the computer's screen the value of a specific element of the array (args [i]). Thus, the program displays the three command-line arguments in the order in which they appeared on the command-line.

For most purposes, a prototypical looping statement can be described as follows (this kind of description shows the *syntax* of the statement):

```
for ( initialisation ; expression ; update ) {
  sequence-of-statements
}
```

where initialisation allows you to declare a loop variable and give it an initial value, expression must yield a boolean value which, if false, stops the loop from looping, and update updates the value of the loop variable each time round the loop (the actual updating is carried out after the execution of the sequence-of-statements that comprise the loop body). The individual statements making up the sequence-of-statements must each be terminated with a semicolon (;).

Exercise 3.3 (Budd, Chapter 4 Exercise 5)

Another useful method provided by the class String is the substring operation. This takes an integer argument, and returns the portion of the string that remains following the index position. For example, if word is a variable containing the string “unhappy”, then word.substring (2) is the string “happy”.

This operation is used in the following program. What will the output be given the command-line argument Sally?

```
static public void main ( String [] args ) {
  String name = args [0];
  String shortName = name.substring (1);
  System.out.println (name + "," + name + ", bo-B" + shortName);
  System.out.println ("Banana-fana Fo-F" + shortName);
  System.out.println ("Fee, Fie, mo-M" + shortName);
  System.out.println (name + "!");
}
```

Solution

Since the command line contains only one String, the argument args of the main method represents an array with one element. That is,

```
args [0] = "Sally"
```

Execution continues with the execution of the individual statements in the body of main.

Statement	Result of execution
String name = args [0];	the variable name refers to the string Sally
String shortName = name.substring (1);	the variable shortName refers to the string ally
System.out.println (name + ", " + ...);	the string Sally, Sally, bo-Bally is output
System.out.println ("Banana-fana ...");	the string Banana-fana Fo-Fally is output
System.out.println ("Fee, Fie, ... ");	the string Fee, Fie, mo-Mally is output
System.out.println (name + "!"):	the string Sally! is output

3.6 Summary of section

Read the summary in Budd, Section 4.6.

4 SUMMARY OF THE UNIT

In this unit you have been introduced to some of the important ideas in software development. You have seen in broad outline how software is developed to meet customers' needs. You have seen that there must be a disciplined approach to software development, particularly for large projects. When developing large projects it is good practice to split the project up into small, manageable parts and, where possible, make use of existing components. Indeed, the whole of the development process should make use of artefacts that have been used before and are known to work, starting with the top-level architecture, and using frameworks, patterns and components wherever possible.

You have seen that large projects must be properly managed if a quality product is to be produced and it is often the lack of good management, and not technical issues, that results in poor quality software.

You have examined the early parts of a case study that will be used to place the major concepts of the course into a real context. The case study will be referred to throughout the course.

You have been introduced to the integrated development environment (IDE) that you will use throughout the course for developing software components in Java.

Finally, you learned to use the IDE to examine your first Java program.

APPENDIX: COMPARING JAVA WITH SMALLTALK

An important prerequisite for M301 is that you should be familiar with an object-oriented programming language before you start the course. There are many such languages, but we expect that the majority of students will have studied Smalltalk in M206. Fundamentally, Smalltalk and Java have a great deal in common but there are differences. We appreciate that the differences between Smalltalk and Java may be a source of confusion early on, particularly when the notation differs and where there are subtle differences in the ways in which the two languages achieve what appear to be the same goals. Therefore, we have provided this short appendix as a way of introducing some of Java's notation by contrasting it with that of Smalltalk. Our aim is to show you that the same basic ideas are present in Java as in Smalltalk but the notation is somewhat different. If you have previously studied an object-oriented language other than Smalltalk you are likely to have less trouble with the notation and reading this appendix should not pose any difficulties.

Probably the most awkward aspect of changing programming language is getting to grips with a different programming environment (the way in which programs are developed). As a rough generalization, when developing a Smalltalk program you have in mind a collection of classes each of which contains a number of methods and you tend to focus on the development of one method at a time. Figure A.1 shows a screen from a typical Smalltalk development environment in which there are four panes: one showing the classes and their inheritance hierarchy, two showing a list of instance variables and a list of methods of a selected class, and a fourth showing the implementation of a selected method.

The focus of attention in a Smalltalk environment is an individual method (but one never loses sight of the context (class) in which the method appears).

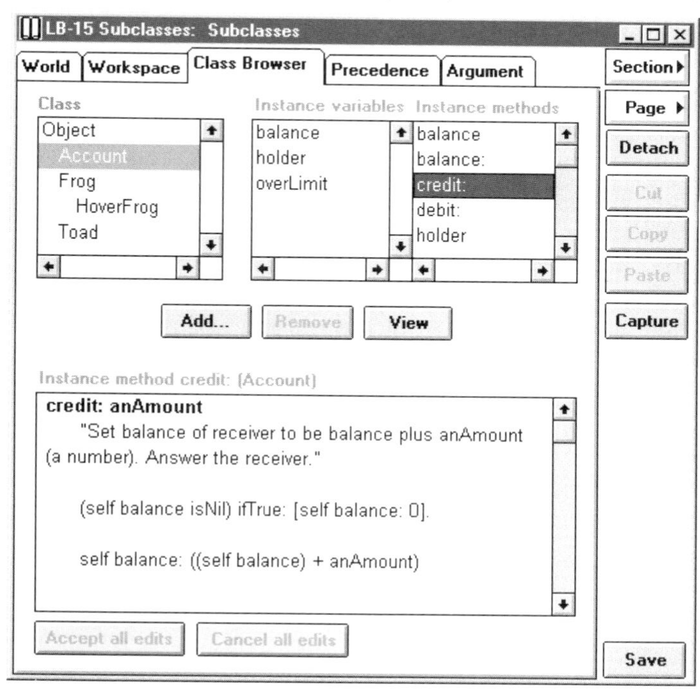

Figure A.1 A Smalltalk development environment

In a typical Java development environment shown in Figure A.2, three significant windows can be identified. On the left-hand side there is the `Project Pane`, which lists the source files associated with the project, and the `Structure Pane`, which lists the members defined in the program chosen in the `Project Pane`. On the right-hand side is the `Content Pane`, which shows the source code of the program chosen in the `Project Pane`.

The tendency in Java development is to focus more on complete classes in which all methods and their implementations are simultaneously displayed.

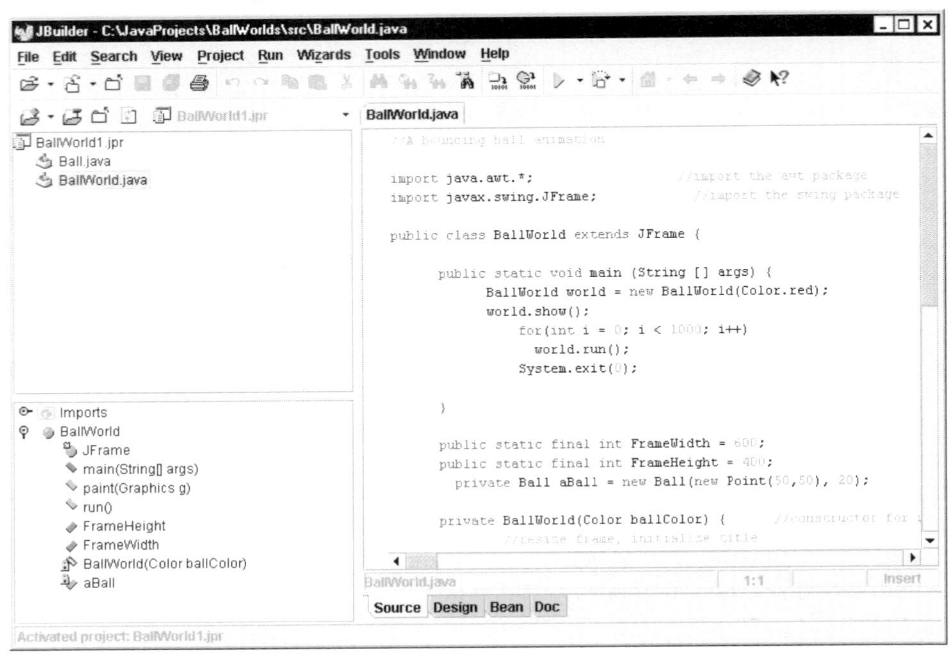

Figure A.2 A Java development environment

When you become familiar with a Smalltalk environment in which methods are the dominant feature, you may find looking at a class as a whole with all its methods and their implementations somewhat distracting. Be assured, however, that the contents of a Java class, which may appear at first sight to be rather complex, is really only a collection of methods and data fields displayed at the same time. A Java program is a collection of classes, and no methods or variables can exist outside a class. The similarities between a Java class and corresponding Smalltalk class are well illustrated in Figure A.3 where an example of a class with similar functionality is given in the two languages. (The text of the Smalltalk class is as it would appear in the Class Reporter of the LearningWorks system in M206.)

A Java class

```
class BankAccount { // implicitly extends
Object
    protected int balance;


// Constructor method

    public BankAccount (int anAmount) {
        balance = anAmount;
    }
// Methods

    public int getBalance () {
        return balance;
    }
    public void setBalance (int anAmount)
{
        balance = anAmount;
    }
    public void deposit (int anAmount) {
        balance = balance + anAmount;
    }
    public void withdrawal (int
    anAmount) {
        if (anAmount <= balance)
            balance = balance - anAmount;
        else
            balance = 0;
    }
    public void transfer (int anAmount,
            BankAccount anAccount) {
        if (balance >= anAmount) {
            anAccount.deposit
    (anAmount);
        balance = balance - anAmount;
        }
    }
}
```

Corresponding Smalltalk class

```
BankAccount subclass of Object
--------------------------------------
instance variables:
    balance
BankAccount class methods
-----------------------------------
new: anAmount
    ^(super new) balance: anAmount

BankAccount instance methods
------------------------------------
balance
    ^balance

balance: anAmount
    balance := anAmount

withdrawal: anAmount
    (anAmount <= balance)
        ifTrue: [balance := balance -
anAmount]
        ifFalse: [balance := 0]


transfer: anAmount to: anAccount
    (balance >= anAmount)
        ifTrue: [anAccount deposit:
anAmount
            balance := balance - anAmount]
```

Figure A.3 The BankAccount class in Java and Smalltalk

Objects and messages

Java is an object-oriented programming language. This implies that a Java program is structured as a community of interacting objects, each of which provides services that are used by other objects of the community. A service is initiated by an object sending a message to the object responsible for providing the service. In Java, this is not usually expressed in terms of message sending but instead by saying that an object invokes a method on another object.

Object-oriented languages have different ways of denoting messages, so one of your major tasks early on in your study of M301 is to come to grips with Java's syntax (the way in which programs are written) which may be quite different from the syntax of the languages you have met before. The following example, taken from the Smalltalk class in Figure A.3,

```
myAccount deposit: 100
```

sends the deposit: message with parameter value 100 to the (receiver) object labelled myAccount. (The effect of this message — to add 100 to the balance of an account — can only be deduced by looking at the method named deposit). In Java, the same effect would be obtained by writing:

```
myAccount.deposit (100)
```

Notice that the same three elements appear in the expression and in the same order, that is, the name of the receiver object, followed by a message, deposit (100), consisting of the name of a method and an argument.

Here is a slightly more complex message expression in Smalltalk which transfers an amount of money from the receiver account to another account:

```
myAccount transfer: 200 to: yourAccount
```

In Java, this could be written as:

```
myAccount.transfer (200, yourAccount)
```

This example illustrates the three main differences between Smalltalk and Java in the syntax of message expressions (known as method calls in Java):

1. the method selector in Smalltalk can consist of several parts, transfer: to:, in Java it is a simple identifier, transfer;
2. in Smalltalk the receiver and the message are separated by a space, in Java they are separated by a full stop (period or dot);
3. the arguments in Smalltalk are separated by parts of the method selector, in Java the arguments are separated by commas and are placed in parentheses. In both cases, the order of arguments is significant.

An important aspect of object-oriented programming is how to set and subsequently retrieve the value of an object's attribute. For example, suppose that you wanted to set the opening balance of an account to 500. In Smalltalk this might be achieved by writing:

```
myAccount balance: 500
```

and retrieving the current balance of an account would typically be achieved by writing:

```
myAccount balance
```

Here, there are two method selectors, balance: and balance. The former sets the value of an attribute, and the latter gets the current value of the attribute. In Java, different identifiers for the two activities could be used:

```
myAccount.setBalance (100)
```

and

```
myAccount.getBalance ()
```

Using set and get as prefixes to the names of such methods is quite common among Java programmers. You might like to note in passing that calls to Java methods that have no arguments must still have the (empty) parentheses present. Again, while the syntax is different in the two languages, the same essential information is present: a receiver object followed by a message consisting of the name of a method with appropriate arguments.

4.1 Creating new objects

To create a new object of the class BankAccount in Smalltalk you could write:

```
myAccount := BankAccount new: 200
```

which would not only create a new object referred to by myAccount, but would also initialize the object with the instance variable balance equal to 200. The method new: is an example of a class method and is defined within the class BankAccount (see Figure A.3). In Java, the same effect would be obtained by writing:

```
myAccount = new BankAccount (200)
```

where **new** is a keyword and the use of the class name BankAccount refers to a constructor method of the class (see Figure A.3). Once again, the created object is initialized with the instance variable, balance, being set to 200.

Sequences of messages

It is usually the case that, to obtain any meaningful computation, a sequence of messages needs to be sent. For example, to open a bank account with an initial balance, then credit the account with some money, followed by the transfer of an amount to another account, and finally record the resulting balance would be achieved in Smalltalk with a message expression *series* such as:

```
myAccount := BankAccount new: 200.
myAccount deposit: 100.
myAccount transfer: 150 to: yourAccount.
myBalance := myAccount balance
```

Here, each message expression is *separated* from the next by a full stop. In Java, the same effect is obtained with a *sequence* of statements each statement containing messages:

```
myAccount = new BankAccount (200);
myAccount.deposit (100);
myAccount.transfer (150, yourAccount);
myBalance = myAccount.balance ();
```

Here, each statement is *terminated* with a semicolon.

In both sequences, the value of the final balance has been returned as the result of sending the message balance to the object myAccount. The identifier myBalance is a reference to the resulting value in both cases (the symbol := is used for assignment in Smalltalk, whereas = is used in Java).

Choosing between actions

A very common requirement in a program is to be able to choose between alternative courses of action. For example, suppose you require a program to debit an account by some given amount provided that there are sufficient funds in the account, but if there are insufficient funds in the account, it will be required to reduce the balance to zero. In Smalltalk, the message ifTrue: ifFalse: is sent to a boolean object as a way of selecting between the two courses of action:

```
(anAmount <= balance)
        ifTrue: [balance := balance - anAmount]
        ifFalse: [balance := 0]
```

where balance is an instance variable. In this example, if the given amount, anAmount, is less than or equal to the current balance, the balance will be reduced by the value of anAmount; otherwise, the current balance is set to zero. This construct has three essential parts: a boolean object (the result of evaluating anAmount <= balance), and two blocks, one of which is evaluated if the boolean object is true, the other being evaluated if the boolean object is false. In Java, the equivalent code is:

```
if (anAmount <= balance) {
   balance = balance - anAmount;
}
else {
   balance = 0;
}
```

The expression that returns the boolean object on which the choice of actions depends is placed in parentheses after the keyword **if**. The set of actions to be performed if the boolean object is true immediately follows the boolean expression and is placed in curly braces. The alternative course of action, also placed in curly braces, follows the keyword **else**.

Repetition of actions

Another common feature of the kind of programming approach used in Smalltalk and Java is called repetition (looping or iteration). That is, a sequence of message expressions (Smalltalk) or a sequence of statements (Java) comprising the body of the loop is to be repeated a number of times. If you know how many repetitions are required, the Java loop construct can be used:

```
for (int i = 0; i < 10; i = i + 1) {
   // body of the loop
}
```

The Java loop construct is introduced by the keyword **for**, which is followed by three expressions separated by semicolons and enclosed in parentheses. These expressions are used (a) to introduce a counter i with an initial value, here, 0, (b) to test a boolean expression prior to each execution of the body of the loop: if the expression returns the true object, the body is executed, otherwise the looping ceases, and (c) to indicate how the counter is modified: here, 1 is added to it after each execution of the body.

In Smalltalk, the same effect would be achieved with the following code:

```
1 to: 10 do: [ ... ]
```

where the block represents the body of the loop.

Methods

A complete method to withdraw an amount of money from an account in Smalltalk (where balance is an instance variable) would be:

```
withdrawal: anAmount
   (anAmount <= balance)
      ifTrue: [balance := balance - anAmount]
      ifFalse: [balance := 0]
```

The Java equivalent is:

```
public void withdrawal (int anAmount) {
   if (anAmount <= balance) {
      balance = balance - anAmount;
   }
   else {
      balance = 0;
   }
}
```

In both languages, anAmount is an argument that refers to the object passed when the method is called. In the case of Smalltalk, the expected argument is a number; in Java it is an integer (denoted by the use of int placed in front of the argument name). In Java, you have to say explicitly what type of object, if any, is returned by the method (nothing is returned in this case, which is indicated by the use of the keyword **void**). This will be discussed further as the course progresses.

Classes

To round off this first look at Java's notation, we shall simply note that, like Smalltalk, a Java program consists of a collection of classes, each of which is a collection of data fields and methods. Precisely how Java classes are constructed will be explained in later sections of the course.

Program execution

In Smalltalk, the way in which a program is executed is very straightforward. You explicitly request an object to be created (always assuming that the class that defines the behaviour of the object has been defined!) and then send a message to it. Thereafter, what happens is dictated by the method that is called. Possibly, this method will cause other objects to be created, again assuming that their classes have already been defined, and will send messages to them.

In Java, the mechanism is slightly different. To begin with, you inform the Java system of the name of the *class* that contains a static method named `main`. The Java system then executes the `main` method which *must* be present in the class you have chosen. The execution of the statements in the `main` method will typically create one or more objects and send messages to them. A word of caution: the precise details of how you tell the Java system which class to begin with will depend upon which program development environment you are using and it may not be obvious that the steps we have outlined actually take place.

Before a Java program can be executed it must be compiled. That is, the Java system must translate the program into another program written in *bytecode* (the program that *you* write is written in what is known as *Java source code* or Java, for short). In performing this translation, the program is checked for a range of errors, and you must correct the errors before the system will execute the program. The process of translation and error checking is known as *compilation* and the software which performs the task is known as a *compiler*. The transformed program, now in bytecode is interpreted. That is, the individual statements of the bytecode program are input to another program known as an interpreter, which examines them and determines what actions the computer must take. In Smalltalk, the same process is used; a program is also compiled into an intermediate code, but this fact is not a step explicitly taken by the developer as it is in Java.

Naming conventions: capitalization

In Java, like Smalltalk, there are conventions about how to construct identifiers (names) and it is quite easy to forget what they are, particularly those relating to the use of upper-case letters. In Java, the main conventions are: the names of classes always begin with an upper-case letter and methods always begin with a lower-case letter. Names of variables used to refer to the objects that you create always begin with a lower-case letter. These conventions are not enforced by the compiler, but are designed to aid the developer. However, it is true that Java is case sensitive; i.e. Java treats lower case '`b`', for example, as different from upper case '`B`'. Consequently, Java would treat the identifier `aBall` and being different from `aball`.

Unit 1.2 Basic Constructs in Java

CONTENTS

STUDY GUIDE

Aims

The aim of this unit is to continue your introduction to Java. In particular, you will learn how to:

- create new objects and send messages to them;
- develop applications using windows;
- use and understand inheritance;
- use Java's event model.

Materials required

For this unit you will require:

1 this course text;
2 the IDE already installed;
3 the *IDE Handbook*;
4 the *Case Study*, Section 2
5 Budd, Chapters 5 and 6.

Required knowledge

It is essential that you are familiar with the material of *Unit 1.1* before attempting this unit. That is, you must know how to create a Java program in the IDE, compile, edit and execute it. You should also know how the constructs, introduced in *Unit 1.1*, are used in writing a simple Java program.

Programme of work

There are three sections to this unit, and on the basis that an evening's work takes between 2½ and 3 hours, this unit should take you five evenings to complete (including answering the associated TMA question). An estimated study plan is given in the following table.

Section	Number of evenings	Materials required
1	1	course text; the IDE, *IDE Handbook*
2	2	course text; the IDE; *IDE Handbook*; Budd, Chapter 5
3	2	course text; the IDE; *IDE Handbook*; the *Case Study*, Section 2; Budd, Chapter 6

Note that Section 1 is a slower-paced introduction to some of the concepts dealt with in Section 2. Therefore, if you get stuck when you are studying Section 2 you should refer back to Section 1 to see whether there is relevant material that could help. Those who feel more confident about their understanding could skip Section 1 altogether since all the concepts introduced in Section 1 are revisited albeit it more rapidly in Section 2.

1 DEVELOPING A SIMPLE JAVA PROGRAM USING JBUILDER 3.5

This section is intended as an introduction to Section 2. All the Java constructs you meet here will be revisited in Section 2. Studying them in this section will give you an opportunity to reinforce them in Section 2. If you are confident of your understanding of Java so far, you may even skip Section 1 without missing any new constructs.

This section contains a set of practical activities that build up a fairly sophisticated Java program in such a way that each step introduces just one or two Java concepts and suggests how you can reinforce your knowledge of them by experimenting with (changing) the program. Each step adds a small amount of additional code so that at the start you can create a single project and thereafter amend the code yourself in small incremental steps. You can, of course, simply read through this text, but in doing so you will not get the benefit of seeing what the code achieves.

The final program is intended to be very similar to the BallWorld program described in Budd, Chapter 5 that you will study in Section 2. If you are confident about your knowledge of Java gained in Unit 1, you can move straight to Section 2, but you will have to get to grips with a fairly complex program and be able to single out the constructs being described from among a number of new ideas. By working through the following practical activities you will be able to concentrate on one or two new ideas at a time and build up your knowledge bit by bit. Our aim in this section is to let you see what certain Java constructs achieve without, at this stage, going into a detailed description of how they do it; this is left until Section 2.

1.1 Objectives

On completing this section you should be able to:

1. create a simple object using a constructor;
2. create and display a window frame on your computer screen;
3. paint a message in a window;
4. use data fields to store simple values;
5. pause the execution of a program using the sleep method from the class Thread;
6. refer to a superclass using the reserved word **super**;
7. build a simple animation using a loop.

1.2 Key terms and concepts

The key terms and concepts associated with this section are:

actual argument
catch
coordinate
constructor
data field
event model
final
for
graphics context
inheritance
try
initialize
interrupt
invoke (a method)
loop
loop control variable
main
paint
pixel
Point
private
protected
public
redefine (a method)
repaint
sleep
static
subclass
super
superclass
Thread

1.3 Study activities, SAQs and solutions

It is assumed that you have already learned how to use the IDE by, for example, working through Sections 1 and 2 of the *IDE Handbook*. It is further assumed that you know that a Java program always starts by executing the body of a main method. In the program below, we have chosen to place the main method in a class of its own named Application. The main method could have been placed in another class in the project but we think that placing it in its own class avoids confusion, at least initially. Having said that, most production Java programs do not separate out the main method (Budd, Chapter 5, Figure 5.2 shows a program written in this way).

Here is a complete Java program that displays an object of the class FirstWorld, named world, on the screen:

```
public class Application {

  public static void main (String [ ] args) {
    FirstWorld world = new FirstWorld();   // create a new FirstWorld object
                                           // named world
    world.show ();                         // display the object on the screen
  }
}
```

When run, this program starts with the execution of the main method. The execution of a main method is known in Java as a thread that, in this example, performs two actions:

- creates an object from the class FirstWorld named world;
- sends the message show to the object world (also known as *invoking the method* show).

An object of the class FirstWorld is a kind of window frame known as a JFrame that has been defined as follows:

```
import javax.swing.*;  // Gives access to the class JFrame and its methods

public class FirstWorld extends JFrame {
            // FirstWorld inherits from Jframe

     // Constructor
  public FirstWorld () {
    setSize (FrameWidth, FrameHeight);
    setTitle ("FirstWorld");
  }

     // Data fields (attributes)
  public static final int FrameWidth = 600;
  public static final int FrameHeight = 400;
}
```

The **import** statement states that this application requires access to the contents of the javax.swing package. The definition of the class JFrame is contained within this package.

The following sequence of practical activities asks you to carry out a number of steps. Following each practical activity is a commentary on the activity and an SAQ which should be attempted immediately after reading the commentary.

> Carry out Practical Activity 3.1 in the *IDE Handbook*.

Practical Activity 1.1

Carry out the following steps.

1 Start up the IDE and access the FirstWorld project created in Practical Activity 3.1 in the *IDE Handbook*.

2 Execute the FirstWorld program to see what happens. You should obtain the window shown in Figure 1.1.

Figure 1.1 The FirstWorld window

3 To stop the application running, click the red Reset button at the bottom left of the JBuilder interface window.

4 Modify the window frame to be a different size and re-run the program.

FirstWorld is a subclass of JFrame (that is, FirstWorld inherits from, or extends, JFrame). An object of the class FirstWorld, world, is a window that has the usual three buttons at the top right-hand corner that minimize, maximize and close the window. The size of the window has been specified by giving values to the JFrame method named setSize, and the window has been given a title specified as an argument to the setTitle method.

When the object world is created by the main method in the Application class, using the new construct, the constructor of FirstWorld is invoked. The constructor initialises the new object by, in this case, setting the size and title of the window.

A **pixel**, short for picture element, is the smallest identifiable part of a screen. It is usually rectangular and can have its colour changed. In this application, the frame is 600 pixels wide and 400 pixels in height. The precise size (measured in cms, say) of the frame on your screen will depend on the resolution of your screen: higher resolution screens have more pixels per unit length.

SAQ 1.1

(a) In the FirstWorld program, objects of which classes have the methods setSize and setTitle?

(b) What does invoking the method show achieve?

(c) What does the statement

```
FirstWorld world = new FirstWorld ();
```

in the main method achieve?

(d) What does it mean to say that a method is *invoked* (or *called*)?

Solution

(a) The methods setSize and setTitle are methods of the class JFrame. They are also methods of the class FirstWorld because FirstWorld inherits from JFrame.

(b) The method show (a method of the class JFrame and hence also of FirstWorld) displays a window frame on the screen.

(c) First, a new object of the class FirstWorld named world is created. Then, the constructor of the class FirstWorld is executed. In this case, the constructor initializes the size and title of the new window frame.

(d) To invoke (or call) a method means to execute the method. (This is the same as saying that a message is sent to an object.)

The FirstWorld class can be modified in a simple way to display, that is, paint, an object in the window. In the following example, a text message is printed in the middle of the window. The shaded area identifies the modifications (additions) that need to be made to the class FirstWorld that was used in Practical Activity 3.1 of the *IDE Handbook*.

```
import javax.swing.*;
import java.awt.*;

public class FirstWorld extends JFrame {
      // Constructor

   public FirstWorld () {
     setSize (FrameWidth, FrameHeight);
     setTitle ("FirstWorld");
   }

      // Data fields (attributes)
   public static final int FrameWidth = 600;
   public static final int FrameHeight = 400;

      // A paint method for drawing a simple string in the FirstWorld window
   public void paint (Graphics g) {
     g.drawString ("A simple message", FrameWidth/2, FrameHeight/2);
   }
}
```

The class JFrame has a method named paint, which clears the window frame and which is automatically invoked (called) by the show method. Since FirstWorld inherits from JFrame, FirstWorld has this same paint method. In this example, we have redefined the paint method so that it simply draws the String object "A simple message" in the middle of the frame.

The additional **import** statement is required because the class Graphics and its method drawString are contained in the java.awt package. A Graphics object, such as g in the example, is known as a *graphics context* and contains a great deal of information that is required in order to paint objects on your computer screen. For example, g will contain information about the font, colour and size of the text drawn by drawString. It is possible to change these attributes using the setter methods of the class Graphics.

Practical Activity 1.2

1 Add the redefined paint method to your existing FirstWorld class.

2 Run the modified application.

3 Change the text of the message.

4 Change the position of the text in the window.

A position within a window is identified by two integers known as *coordinates*. The first integer (the *x-coordinate*) is the number of pixels that the required position is from the left-hand edge of the window. The second integer (the *y-coordinate*) is the number of pixels down from the top of the window. The top left-hand corner of a window has coordinates (0, 0), as shown in Figure 1.2, and is known as the **origin** of the coordinates. A general point P is denoted by $P(x, y)$, as shown in Figure 1.2, where x represents the distance from the origin in the x-direction and y represents the distance in the y-direction. The position with coordinates (FrameWidth/2, FrameHeight/2) is in the middle of the window.

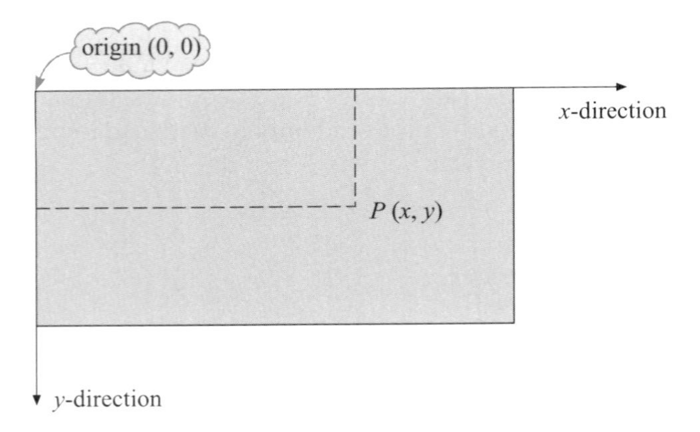

Figure 1.2 x- and y-coordinates in a window

Note that the title of the window (set using setTitle) and the three buttons are placed in a horizontal strip across the top of the window. It is the top left-hand corner of this strip that has the coordinates (0, 0).

5 Amend the paint method to use the following statement to change the colour of the text.

```
g.setColor(Color.green);
```

Redefining an inherited method means that objects of the subclass (FirstWorld in this example) use the newly defined version of the method. So, when the main method in the Application class is invoked, and the following statements are executed:

```
FirstWorld world = new FirstWorld (); // create a new FirstWorld object
                                      // named world
world.show ();                        // show (display) the object on the screen
```

the object world (an instance of the class FirstWorld) is sent the method show (inherited from JFrame) which will use the redefined paint method.

SAQ 1.2

(a) What does the paint method specify?

(b) Why is it necessary to provide the paint method with an argument from the class Graphics?

(c) What is meant by the phrase, 'to redefine a method'?

(d) Under what conditions can you redefine a method?

(e) Why would the statement:

```
g.drawString ("Hello", 5, 5);
```

result in no text being displayed?

Solution

(a) The paint method specifies which graphics objects are to be painted in the window frame.

(b) An object from the class Graphics (such as g in the example) is known as a graphics context and provides information about how a graphics object is to be displayed on the screen.

(c) To redefine a method means to provide a new body (set of statements) for an existing method.

(d) You can only redefine inherited methods.

(e) The statement is attempting to display the text in the same area that is occupied by the window title.

The next example contains a 'cosmetic' change to the previous version of FirstWorld. It introduces two private *data fields* (also known as attributes or instance variables) named xCoord and yCoord. These instance variables will hold the *x*- and *y*-coordinates of the position at which the simple message is to start.

```
import javax.swing.*;
import java.awt.*;

public class FirstWorld extends JFrame {

  public FirstWorld () {
    setSize (FrameWidth, FrameHeight);
    setTitle ("FirstWorld");
  }

  public static final int FrameWidth = 600;
  public static final int FrameHeight = 400;

  private int xCoord = FrameWidth/2;
  private int yCoord = FrameHeight/2;

  public void paint (Graphics g) {
    g.drawString ("A simple message", xCoord, yCoord);
  }
  }
```

Practical Activity 1.3

1 Amend your existing FirstWorld class as shown above.

2 Run the modified application.

3 Change the initial values of the new data fields and re-run the program.

Data fields, used to store values or reference objects, can be used anywhere within the class in which they are declared. When they are declared, as in

```
private int xCoord = FrameWidth/2;
private int yCoord = FrameHeight/2;
```

they can be given initial values. Subsequently, within the body of a method in the same class, they can be given new values (we shall use this fact in the next practical activity).

Every object of the class FirstWorld will contain these two data fields.

You will learn later that, when there is a possibility that other classes may be defined as inheriting from a class like FirstWorld, it may be more appropriate to declare data fields as **protected**.

The reason we have declared these data fields as **private** means that they cannot be accessed (referred to) outside the class FirstWorld. It is always a good idea to declare data fields and methods as **private** when you are certain that they are not required outside the class in which they are declared.

When used in the call to drawString,

```
g.drawString("A simple message", xCoord, yCoord);
```

the data fields are being used as *actual arguments*. That is, the values of the data fields are being passed to the method drawString and determine the location of the start of the string in the window.

In FirstWorld, there are four data fields: FrameWidth, FrameHeight, xCoord and yCoord. The first two are declared as **public static final**, the last two are declared as **private**. A **private** data field can be accessed only within the class in which it is declared whereas a **public** data field can be accessed within other classes too. A data field declared as **static** is a class data field (also known as a class variable). That is, there is only one instance of the data field, which is shared by all the objects of the class. If a data field is *not* declared as **static**, each object of the class has its own copy of the data field. A data field declared as **final** represents a constant (not a variable) because its value, once set, cannot be changed.

SAQ 1.3

(a) What is a data field?

(b) What is a data field used for?

(c) How would you arrange for a data field to be shared by all the objects of a class?

Solution

(a) A data field is a variable (or constant if declared as final). Each object of the class in which a data field occurs has such a variable (or constant).

(b) A data field is used to store a value or a reference to an object, and can be used anywhere within the class in which it is declared.

(c) You would declare the data field to be **static**.

The following modification of the FirstWorld class places two copies of the same object on different parts of the window at different times and provides the illusion of a simple movement. This requires the following sequence of three actions:

display the message at some part of the window;

wait for a few seconds;

display the message at some other part of the window.

To execute this sequence of actions we shall introduce a new method, named run, to do this. Thus, the main method will first display the window, using show as before, and will then call run to perform the remaining actions.

```
public class Application {
  public static void main (String [ ] args) {
    FirstWorld world = new FirstWorld (); // create a new FirstWorld object named
                                          // world
    world.show ();                        // show (display) the object on the screen
    world.run ();                         // perform other actions with the world object
  }
}
```

The FirstWorld class contains a new method named run (shown shaded).

```
import javax.swing.*;
import java.awt.*;

public class FirstWorld extends JFrame {
  public FirstWorld () {
    setSize (FrameWidth, FrameHeight);
    setTitle ("FirstWorld");
  }

  public static final int FrameWidth = 600;
  public static final int FrameHeight = 400;
```

```
    private int xCoord = FrameWidth/2;
    private int yCoord = FrameHeight/2;

    public void paint (Graphics g) {
      g.drawString ("A simple message", xCoord, yCoord);
    }

    public void run () {
      try {
        Thread.sleep (3000);                      // stop the execution for 3 seconds
      } catch (Exception e) {System.exit (0);}
      xCoord = 25;                                // set the coordinates to new values
      yCoord = 100;
      repaint ();                                 // repaint the window
    }
}
```

Practical Activity 1.4

Continue the modification of the FirstWorld class, which was started above, by carrying out the following steps.

1 Amend your existing FirstWorld class as shown above.

2 Run the modified application.

3 Amend the run method by adding another three second sleep and paint the message a third time at some new position. Re-run the program.

4 What happens to the messages that are already displayed in the window whenever a new message appears?

This modification has introduced two new ideas:

- the use of the sleep method to pause processing;
- the use of the method repaint.

The sleep method takes a single argument expressing the number of milliseconds for which the execution of the program (also known as a thread) should pause. In Java, it is possible to construct applications that consist of several threads (separate programs) that interact, that is, they send messages to one another. This may mean that one thread may wish to 'wake up' a sleeping thread before the normal end of its sleep. Such a rude awakening is technically known as an *interrupt* and is dealt with through Java's exception handling mechanism that you will study later. For now, simply accept that whenever you use the sleep method it must appear within a **try** statement as shown in the above example. If an exception does occur while the thread sleeps, the **catch** part of the **try** statement will be executed. In this case, the thread simply stops (the System method exit is called).

At first sight, it may seem rather strange to have used the method repaint when what we really want is to invoke paint again. To understand why repaint is required, you need to know a little about Java's *event model* and how Java deals with output to your computer's screen.

We begin by explaining the programming mechanism that you have to use. Repainting the screen in Java is a two-stage process. First, you call repaint and then repaint calls paint for you. In fact, when you invoke the method show, in the main method, show actually calls repaint: you cannot call paint directly. So, when you wish to change the contents of a window, you should always call repaint (although you must specify what has to be done in the method paint — suitably redefined in your new class).

The reason for this apparently bizarre process is the special role of repaint. The repaint method does not invoke paint straight away: it causes the call to paint to be added to an event queue to await its turn to be executed. Java deals with a large number of different kinds of events, as you will discover in due course, and must ensure that they are all dealt with in an organized way.

Since painting the screen is a relatively slow process — certainly much, much slower than the speed at which the processor operates — it is more efficient to place the painting operation in a queue to await its turn while the processor is allowed to get on with other tasks. For example, the processor could swap over to executing another thread while the painting of the screen required by the previous thread takes place (this is an example of concurrency that you will study in Block 2).

SAQ 1.4

(a) What does the method sleep do? Of which class is sleep a method? What special action do you have to take in order to use sleep?

(b) What action does repaint take when invoked?

Solution

(a) The method sleep causes the program (thread) in which it appears to stop executing for a number of milliseconds specified by its argument. It is a method of the Thread class. It must be invoked within a **try** statement and you must specify (in a **catch** part) what action is to be taken if an exception arises while the thread is sleeping.

(b) The method repaint adds a call to paint to an event queue.

In the previous example, the simple message(s) stayed on the screen each time a new message was added. The following simple amendment to the paint method clears the window before repainting it.

```
public void paint (Graphics g) {
  super.paint (g);          // invokes the paint method of JFrame
  g.drawString ("A simple message", xCoord, yCoord);
}
```

Practical Activity 1.5

1 Amend your existing FirstWorld class as shown above.

2 Run the modified application.

The statement

```
super.paint(g);        // invokes the paint method of Jframe
```

invokes the paint method of the class JFrame which simply clears the window. The special word **super** is used to refer to the superclass (JFrame is the superclass of FirstWorld, and FirstWorld is the class in which this statement occurs).

You will realize that, in this example, there are (at least) two methods named paint: there is one in the class JFrame (that clears the window) and one in FirstWorld (that draws the message) and they are distinguished by prefixing the paint method from the superclass with the keyword **super**.

SAQ 1.5

To what does the reserved word super refer? Why is it needed?

Solution

The keyword super refers to the superclass of the class in which it is used. In this example, it is used within the class FirstWorld and so refers to the class JFrame. It is required when a method is redefined in order to distinguish between two methods with the same name: the original method in the superclass and the redefined method in the subclass.

In the next example, we shall introduce some simple animation in which the message will appear to move across the window. This is achieved by painting the message at one position, clearing the window, and repainting the message at another position, and then repeating the whole process a number of times.

The only new idea required is that of a loop. The run method simply sleeps for 1 second, calculates a new position of the message, and repaints the message. It repeats this sequence 10 times using a **for** loop.

```
public void run () {
   for (int i = 0; i < 10; i++) {
      try {
         Thread.sleep (1000);
      } catch (Exception e) {System.exit (0);}
      xCoord = xCoord + 40;
      yCoord = yCoord + 25;
      repaint();
   }
}
```

The expression i++ is a shorthand for the assignment i = i + 1.

Practical Activity 1.6

1 Amend your existing FirstWorld class as shown above.

2 Run the modified application.

3 Amend the run method so that the message moves horizontally across the window.

4 Reduce the time that the thread sleeps between individual movements.

A **for** loop is a programming control structure that enables one or more statements (collectively known as a block) to be executed repeatedly a given number of times.

The **for** loop used in the practical activity has the following form.

```
for (int i = 0; i < 10; i++) {
   // a block of statements
}
```

Following the **for** keyword is a specification of the number of repetitions of the loop. First, a loop control variable is declared (int i) and given an initial value (0). Every time the loop is executed i is incremented by 1 (i++). Provided the value of the loop control variable i remains less than 10 (i < 10) the statements will be repeated. In this example, the loop will be repeated precisely 10 times.

The block of statements to be repeated is placed inside braces, { and }. If only one statement is to be repeated, the braces are not required. The block of statements to be repeated is also known as 'the body of the loop'.

The amount by which the loop control variable can be increased each time the loop is repeated can be more complicated than simply adding 1 each time. Similarly, the condition for stopping the loop (i < 10, in the above) can be a more complicated expression. In the following example, the loop control variable is incremented by 3 each time the loop is repeated, and the loop stops repeating once the loop control variable is no longer smaller than 12.

```
for (int j = 1; j < 3*4; j = j + 3) {...}
```

This loop repeats 4 times; the values of the loop control variable (j) each time round the loop are 1, 4, 7, and 10.

SAQ 1.6

What is a **for** loop used for? What is a control variable and what is it used for?

Solution

A **for** loop is used to repeat a block of one or more statements a number of times. The loop control variable is an integer variable that is incremented each time the block is repeated and is used to determine the number of repetitions of the block. The loop stops repeating once the condition in the loop heading becomes false.

In this final example, we shall animate a graphical object rather than a text object. The object will be a coloured disk. The first task is to develop a class to represent the disk object. We shall start by describing the attributes (data fields) required to represent a disk on the screen. Figure 1.3 shows a disk at a typical position within a window frame.

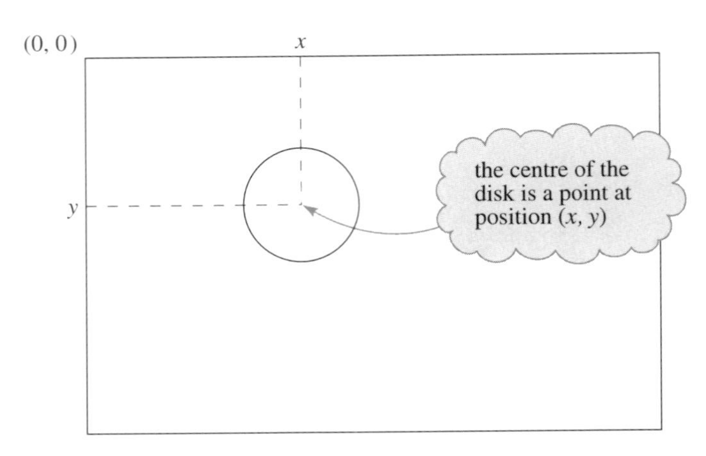

Figure 1.3 A disk in a window frame.

A disk is characterised by:

- the position of its centre in the window;
- its radius;
- its colour.

There is a class in the Java package awt named Point whose objects represent points in a window frame. Each point is represented by its distance from the left-hand edge of the frame (the x value, measured in pixels) and the distance from the top edge of the window (the y value, also measured in pixels).

Here is a class that describes the disk objects:

```
import java.awt.*;

public class Disk {
   protected Point location; // position of disk in window
   protected int radius;     // radius of disk
   protected Color color;    // colour of disk

   public Disk (Point p, int r, Color c) { // initialise disk
      location = p;
      radius = r;
      color = c;
   }

   public Point getLocation () {
      return location;
   }

   public void setLocation (Point p) {
      location = p;
   }

   public void paint (Graphics g) {
      g.setColor (color);
      g.fillOval (location.x – radius, location.y – radius, 2*radius, 2*radius);
   }
}
```

Here is the FirstWorld class suitably modified to deal with a Disk object.

```
import javax.swing.*;      // for JFrame
import java.awt.*;         // for Graphics and Point

public class FirstWorld extends JFrame {

  public FirstWorld () {
    setSize (FrameWidth, FrameHeight);
    setTitle ("FirstWorld");
  }

  public static final int FrameWidth = 600;
  public static final int FrameHeight = 400;

  private int xCoord = 25;   // set the initial values of the coordinates
  private int yCoord = 100;  // near the top left-hand corner of the window frame

     // create a new point object at this specific location
  private Point p = new Point (xCoord, yCoord);
     // create a (red) disk object, of radius 15, initially at the location p
  private Disk d = new Disk (p, 15, Color.red);

  public void run () {
    for (int i = 0; i < 10; i++) {
      try {
        Thread.sleep (500);
      } catch (Exception e) { System.exit(0); }
      xCoord = xCoord + 25;  // change the value of xCoord by a small amount
      yCoord = yCoord + 25;  // change the value of yCoord by a small amount
      p.setLocation (xCoord, yCoord);  // set new coordinates for point
      d.setLocation (p);  // set the position of the disc to new coordinates given
by p
      repaint ();
    }
  }
     // A paint method for drawing a disk in the FirstWorld window
  public void paint (Graphics g) {
    super.paint(g);
    d.paint (g);
  }
}
```

Practical Activity 1.7

1. Amend your existing FirstWorld class as shown above.
2. Use the Class Wizard to add a new class named Disk to the FirstWorld project (see Practical Activity 2.2 in the *IDE Handbook*). Type in the Disk class given above.
3. Run the modified application.
4. Amend the run method so that the disk moves more smoothly. That is, reduce the amount by which the disk moves each time (you should also increase the number of repetitions of the **for** loop to ensure that the disk moves the same total distance across the window).
5. Reduce the time that the thread sleeps between individual movements.

The technique used in this practical activity uses a Point object to represent the location of the centre of the disk. By altering the values of the two coordinates, xCoord and yCoord, by a small amount each time round the loop and setting the Point to the new position, the location of the disk changes.

Both the Point class and the Disk class have a method named setLocation that re-sets the location of the respective object in the window frame.

A Disk object has three data fields that specify the location of its centre (as a point), the size of its radius (given as a number of pixels) and its colour. The Disk constructor sets the initial values of these data fields. They have been declared as **protected** which means that they can be accessed within other classes, but only those that extend (inherit from) Disk. If you are unsure whether a data field will only be used by the class in which it is declared, it is better to declare it **protected** rather than **private**.

A Disk object's behaviour consists of three methods: getLocation and setLocation (to return and set the location of the disk's centre, respectively), and paint (to paint the disk on the window).

The paint method of Disk uses the Graphics method fillOval,

```
g.fillOval (location.x – radius, location.y – radius, 2*radius, 2*radius);
```

which has four arguments, that specify the position and size of a rectangle in which the oval shape will be painted as illustrated in Figure 1.4. The position of the top left-hand corner of the rectangle is calculated from the position of the centre of the disk (location.x, location.y) where x and y are the names of data fields that store the *x*-coordinate and *y*-coordinate of a Point object, respectively. The width and height of the rectangle are both twice the size of the radius of the disk.

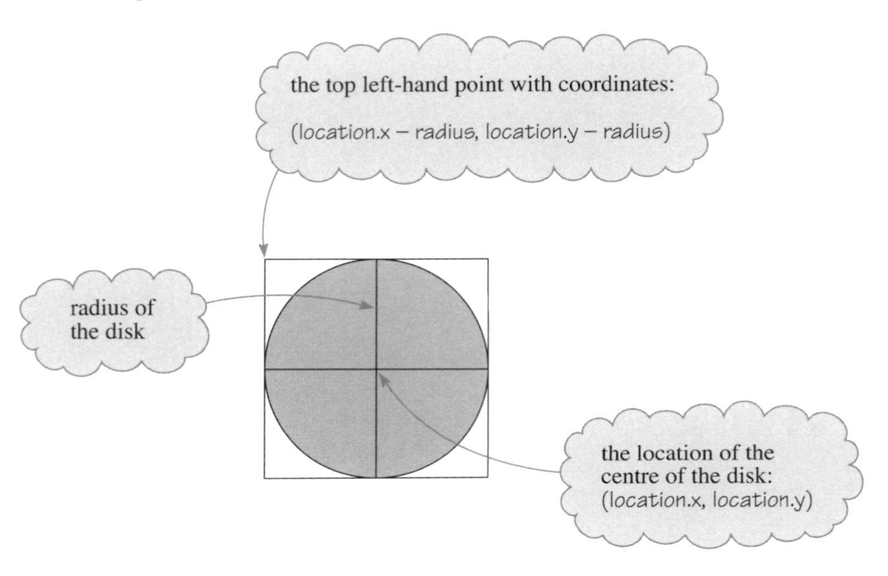

Figure 1.4 Painting a circular shape

1.4 Summary of section

In this section you have been introduced to a number of Java features in preparation for your study of the next section. These include:

1. how to draw a window on your computer screen;
2. how to paint a simple text message to a window using the drawString method;
3. how to use data fields (instance variables) to hold data;
4. how to paint two copies of a simple text message at different times on a window to give the illusion of movement using the paint and repaint methods;
5. how to cause a program to pause its execution for a specified time using the sleep method;
6. how to use a **for** loop to repeat the painting of a text message to give a simple animation effect;
7. how to produce a simple animation of a simple object.

2 BALL WORLDS: SWING CLASSES, CONSTRUCTORS AND INHERITANCE

In *Unit 1.1*, Section 3 you were introduced to the basic constructs of Java including message passing, classes, data members, methods, public and static modifiers, and the role of the main method. This section continues this process by examining in more detail the Java constructs introduced in Section 1 that deal with:

- the creation of a new object;
- the creation of applications that make use of windows;
- inheritance.

If at any stage in reading this section you find it difficult to understand what is being said, you may find it useful to review the corresponding discussion in Section 1.

2.1 Objectives

On completing this section you should be able to:

1. create a small application that uses the Abstract Windowing Toolkit (AWT) and Swing packages to simulate movement in a window based on the Java graphics model;
2. develop Java programs with several classes using inheritance;
3. define and use object constructors;
4. define constants in Java;
5. represent a simple Java program as a class diagram;
6. construct a Java program by accessing code held in files.

2.2 Key terms and concepts

The important terms and concepts associated with this section are:

accessor methods	debugging	interface class
actual argument	formal argument	new
application class	frame (window)	object initialization
argument passing	framework	object creation
class diagram	graphics model	package
constants	implementation class	Swing classes
constructor	inheritance	this

2.3 Study activities

Your main task in this section is to read Budd, Chapter 5. This chapter uses a program named BallWorld to explain a number of Java concepts. The first activity is designed to show you what this program does and should be attempted *before* you start reading Budd, Chapter 5.

1. Ensure that you have completed Practical Activity 3.1 in the *IDE Handbook*, and then attempt Exercise 3.1 in Section 3 of the *IDE Handbook*, which involves importing, compiling and running the BallWorld program. Attempt SAQ 2.1.
2. Read Budd, Chapter 5 up to the end of Section 5.5 remembering to attempt the relevant SAQs in Section 2.4.
3. Carry out the remaining practical activities in Section 3 of the *IDE Handbook*, which involve importing, compiling, debugging and running the MultiBallWorld program.
4. Read Budd, Section 5.6.
5. At the end of each section of Budd, Chapter 5, attempt the relevant SAQ (it is labelled with the same number as the section).
6. When you have read Budd, Chapter 5, study Example 2.1 below, which shows a class diagram for the BallWorld program.
7. Finally, when you have completed the above, attempt the exercises in Subsection 2.5 and check whether any other exercises from Budd, Chapter 5 are included in the TMA for this unit.

Explanatory notes

1 The **new** expression (Budd, Figure 5.2)

Line 5 of the BallWorld class contains the statement:

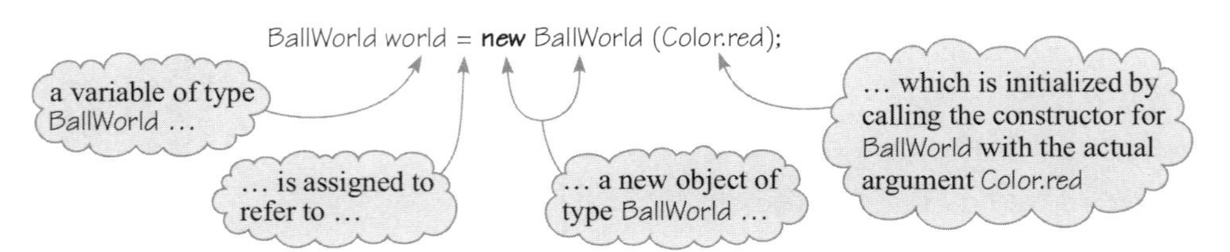

Figure 2.1

On the right-hand side of the = symbol is a **new** expression

new BallWorld (Color.red);

which, when executed, has two effects:

1. it creates a new (uninitialized) object (of type BallWorld, in this example);
2. it initializes the new object by invoking BallWorld's constructor using the argument(s) supplied in parentheses (in this case, Color.red).

The second step, initialization, is carried out automatically by the Java run-time system that invokes the appropriate constructor with the given arguments. It is for this reason that Budd states, 'the user will never directly execute a constructor'.

On the left-hand side of the = symbol is the declaration of a variable named world whose type is BallWorld.

Hence, the meaning of the complete statement on line 5 is:

> create a new object of type BallWorld, initialized using the constructor, and assign it to the variable, world.

You can see another use of the **new** expression on line 13 of Budd, Figure 5.2 where the variable aBall is assigned to a new object of type Ball. The definition of the constructor for Ball appears in the class Ball shown in Budd, Figure 5.3.

2 Calling methods and argument passing (Budd, Figure 5.2)

To see what happens when the system executes the BallWorld constructor on line 5 of Budd, Figure 5.2, note first that Color.red is an instance of the class Color representing the colour red. This value is passed to the BallWorld constructor where it is assigned to the formal argument named ballColor as indicated by the thick arrow in Figure 2.2 below.

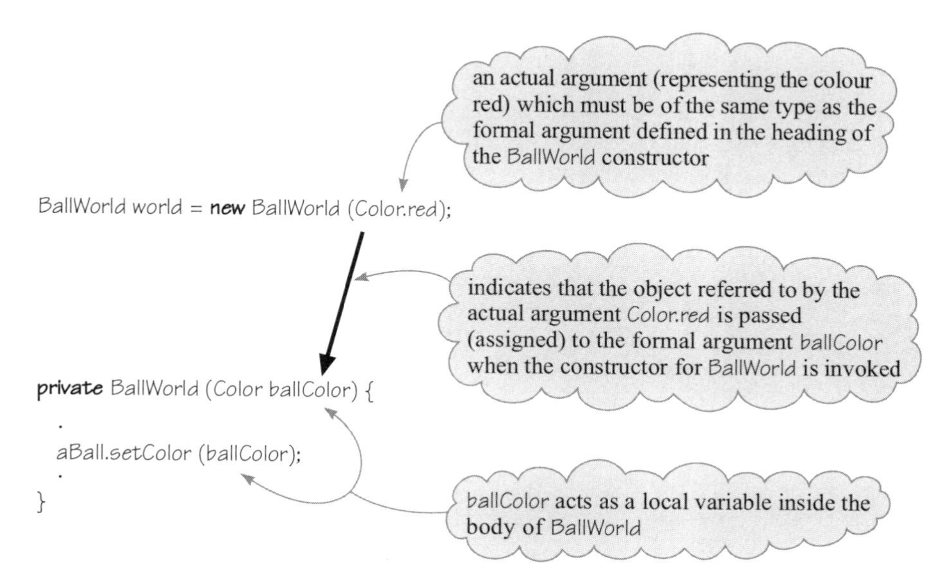

Figure 2.2 Argument passing

This mechanism for argument passing is used for method calls as well as for constructors.

On line 19, the object referred to by ballColor is passed to the setColor function as shown in Figure 2.3.

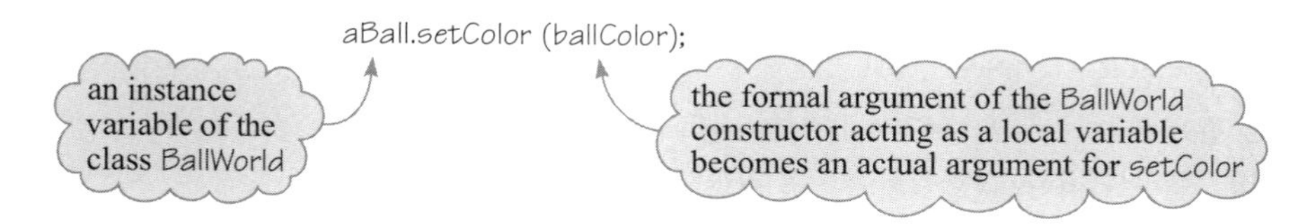

Figure 2.3 The value of ballColor is passed to setColor

The setColor method is defined in the class Ball as in Figure 2.4.

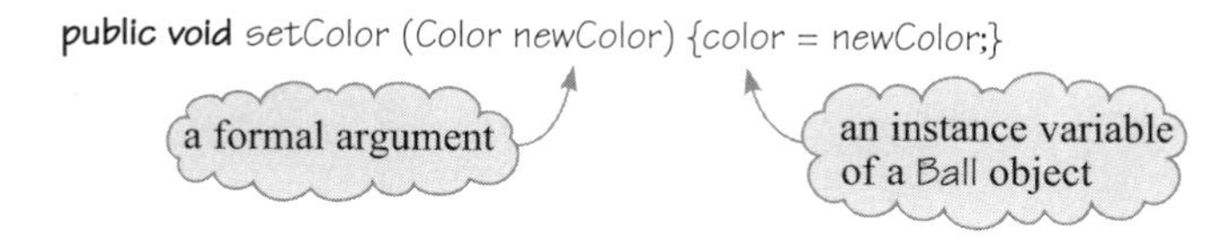

Figure 2.4 The setColor method

The effect of executing setColor is to assign the value of the formal argument newColor (obtained from ballColor) to the instance variable color. Subsequently, the value stored in the instance variable color is used by the paint procedure defined in the Ball class (see Budd, Figure 5.3):

```
g.setColor (color);
```

Here, setColor (color) is a method call known to objects of type Graphics (which is different from the method call of the same name known to Ball objects) which interprets the value of color in such a way that, in this example, a red oval is drawn on the computer's screen.

3 Objects and references (Budd, Figure 5.2)

To understand objects and references, we shall examine what happens to a ball object in the class BallWorld. The object is first defined in the following line:

```
private Ball aBall = new Ball(new Point(50,50), 20);
```

The object, aBall, is defined using the constructor of class Ball (see Budd, Figure 5.3). The constructor makes a ball that includes two data fields: loc which is a reference to an object of the Point class and rad which is of a simple integer data type (in this case, 20). At this stage, aBall can be pictured as shown in Figure 2.5.

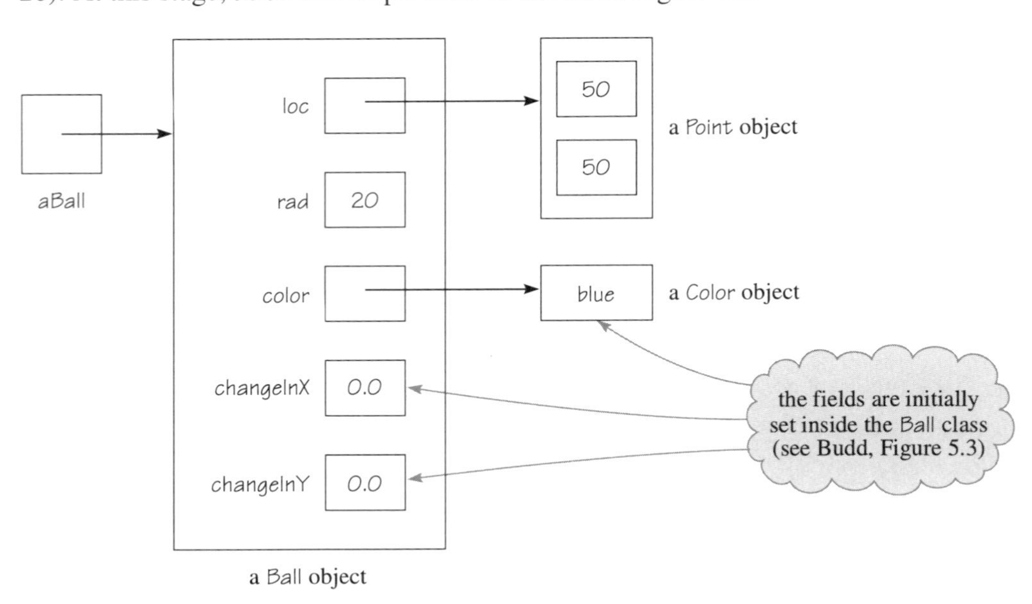

Figure 2.5 An initialized Ball object

An alternative definition for the class Ball could have included a constructor that would enable the color and motion to be initialized as part of the construction process, but the decision was taken to leave color and motion setting as separate activities.

Notice that because the location is a point, which is an object, loc is a reference to a Point object. However, since rad is a simple integer, which is not considered an object in Java, the value is contained within the data field itself. At the same time, the data fields color, changeInX and changeInY are initialized to blue, 0.0 and 0.0, respectively. (Notice that changeInX and changeInY are simple data types and ballColor is an object.)

Inside the constructor for BallWorld (see Figure 5.3) the ball referenced by aBall is subject to the following two method calls.

```
aBall.setColor(ballColor);
aBall.setMotion(3.0, 6.0);
```

After these two method calls, the state of the ball is given in Figure 2.6.

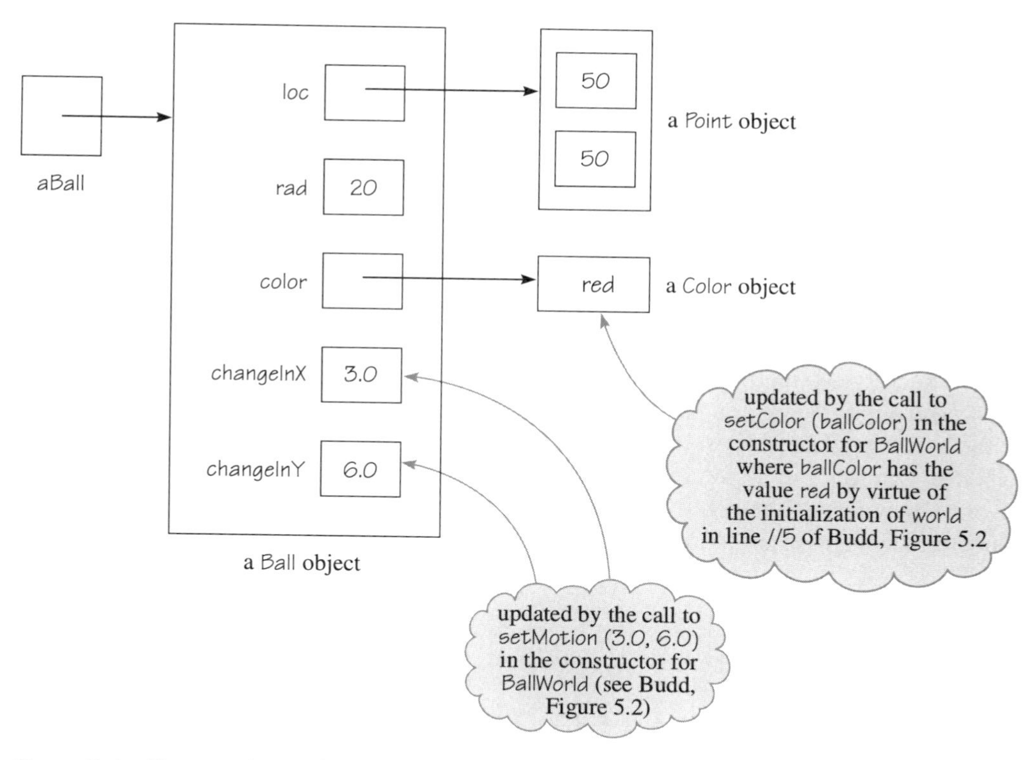

Figure 2.6 The Ball object after two setter messages

The next thing that happens is the execution of a run method. The result of the execution is that the location is translated by the values of motion. So the state after an execution of run is shown in Figure 2.7.

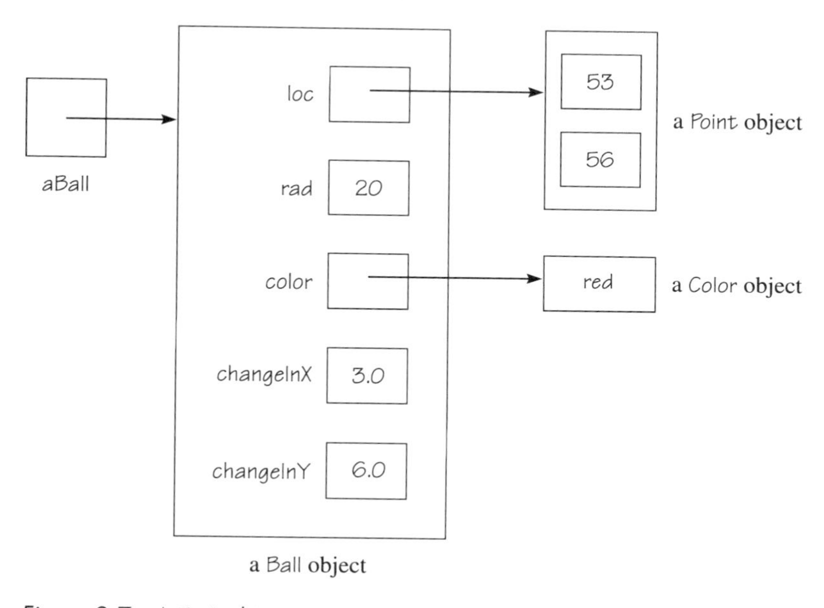

Figure 2.7 A Ball object

4 Java windows (Budd, Figure 5.2)

The view that the Java run-time system takes of a graphical window on the computer's screen is that it is a rectangular shape with a specified width and height. As a programmer, you will want to place various graphical objects into the window at specific places. To do this you need to know a little about the geometry of a window. A discussion of this is given in Practical Activity 1.1 in Section 1 of this unit.

In the BallWorld class, the window has a width of 600 and a height of 400 pixels. This means that any point within the boundary of the window must have an *x*-value between 0 and 600, and a *y*-value between 0 and 400. Therefore, the point in the middle of the window will have coordinates (300, 200).

It is a convention, used in the book and adopted throughout this course, to start the identifiers which represent constants, such as FrameWidth and FrameHeight, with an upper-case letter.

5 What? No receiver object? (Budd, Figure 5.2)

BallWorld inherits from JFrame and JFrame inherits from Frame. In Budd, Figure 5.2, lines 16 and17, two methods, setSize and setTitle, are used. These methods are inherited from the class Frame. However, in neither case is there an explicit receiver for the message. The purpose of these methods is to set the size and title of the BallWorld window initialized by the BallWorld constructor. That is, they apply to the current object being initialized. To denote the current object, Java uses the reserved identifier, **this**, and lines 16 and 17 could have been written as follows.

```
this.setSize (FrameWidth, FrameHeight);
this.setTitle ("Ball World");
```

However, in cases where there is no confusion, Java allows you to omit **this**.

6 The operator || (Budd, Figure 5.2)

The symbol || stands for the boolean operator 'or'. We shall discuss this in *Unit 1.3*, Section 1.

7 Rectangles, ovals and balls (Budd, Figure 5.3)

In Java, the easiest way to draw solid objects such as circles, ovals, squares and rectangles on your screen is to create a window and then use the facilities of the Graphics class. This class, provided as part of the Java run-time library, contains many useful methods such as fillOval. The fillOval method takes four arguments that define a rectangular area in a window. They are (see Figure 2.8):

- the two coordinates of the top left-hand corner of the rectangle;
- the width of the rectangle;
- the height of the rectangle.

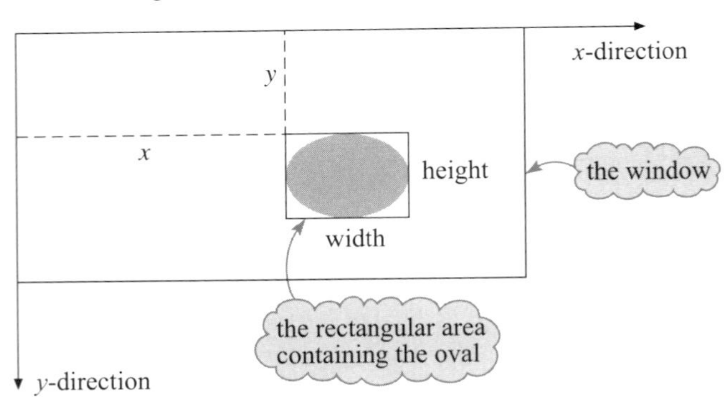

Figure 2.8 The arguments defining an oval shape in a window

The fillOval method then fits an oval shape with a specified colour into the rectangular area. The same method can be used to draw circles by making the width and height of the rectangular area the same.

In line 13 of the BallWorld class, a new Ball is created which is described in terms of a point located at position (x, y) = (50, 50) and radius rad = 20. The Ball paint method contains the statement,

```
g.fillOval (loc.x – rad, loc.y – rad, 2*rad, 2*rad);
```

which creates an oval within a rectangle, whose top left-hand corner is at position (30, 30) and whose width and height are both 40 (that is, it is a square). The quantities loc.x and loc.y are the *x*- and *y*-coordinates of the Point loc. Thus, the dimensions of a ball are represented in the program as a rectangle which, in this case, is a square! However, this square will not be painted on the screen, instead a filled circle of a size that fits into the square is painted.

8 Moving objects on the screen (Budd, Figure 5.3)

Once the circle representing a ball is painted on the screen, movement is obtained by continually

- changing, by a small amount, the coordinates of the Point loc which defines the centre of the ball,
- repainting the window with the circle in its new position.

In the Ball class, this is achieved by the method moveTo via the use of the move method applied to loc (move is a method defined in the class Point).

9 Moving windows about the screen

Once you execute the BallWorld program, you will obtain a window (frame) on your computer screen on which a ball (a red filled circle) moves around, 'bouncing' off the sides of the window. You will be able to move the window (by dragging, using your mouse) while the ball continues to move. However, if you resize the window (by dragging one of its sides, for example) the simulation does not automatically resize to fit the new size of the window. This is because the window was created with fixed (constant) values for its width and height (see lines 11 and 12 of the class BallWorld). Using the computer's ability to resize a window does not affect the BallWorld program, which continues to draw the circle within a fixed region only part of which is displayed on the screen. It is possible to rectify this problem by defining FrameWidth and FrameHeight as variables, asking the operating system, from time to time, for the current size of the window, and modifying these variables accordingly. Alternatively, the problem may be solved by using the setResizeable method from the class Frame to prevent the user from resizing the window.

10 Graphics objects (Budd, Section 5.4)

The graphics object, named g, which appears as an argument to the paint method in Ball and the paint method in BallWorld, is supplied by the Java system customized for the particular platform (the hardware and operating system) on which the program is running. A graphics object enables you to draw graphical objects on the screen and has a number of data fields, such as color, which specify how the graphical object is to appear (or be rendered) on the screen. So, for example, the statement, aBall.paint (g), means, 'paint a representation of the object referred to by aBall on the screen using the information supplied by the graphics object g'. For the present, simply accept that you require a graphics object as an argument to the paint method.

11 The paint and repaint methods (Budd, Section 5.4)

There is an important interaction between the paint and repaint methods, which does not follow the usual sequential programming language paradigm. This is an example of Java's event model that you will study in more detail in Section 3 and *Unit 1.3*. To see how paint and repaint interact read the commentary that follows Practical Activity 1.4 in Section 1 of this unit.

12 Flow of control (Figure 5.2)

The BallWorld class shown in Budd, Figure 5.2 operates as follows. The work of any application begins with the execution of a main method. In BallWorld, this consists of creating a BallWorld object, referred to by the variable world, and invoking the method show on it. The method show uses a method named paint in order to display the world object on the screen. The design of the paint method (inside the class BallWorld) is such that it first calls the paint method in the superclass (JFame) to clear the window and then paints a ball object (line 23). The main method then goes on to invoke the run method 1000 times before the System method exit is called to stop the execution of the program.

13 The operator ++ (Budd, Figure 5.2)

In the BallWorld main method, the following for statement occurs:

```
for (int i = 0; i < 1000; i++)
```

The expression i++ is a shorthand for the assignment i = i + 1.

14 Java 2 and Swing classes (Budd, Section 5.3, Footnote 2)

Java 2 Platform a registered trademark of Sun MicroSystem Inc.

The **Java platform** is the predefined set of Java classes in the installation, which are contained in packages delivering graphics, input/output, networking, user interfaces, security and more. The Java platform is also referred to as the Java runtime environment or the core Java APIs (application programming interfaces).

We use the Java 2 Platform on this course. *Java 2 Platform* is a term trademarked by Sun for marketing purposes. However, programmers usually refer to the Java platform by its official version number, which is 1.2.2 for this course.

One significant addition in Java 2 is a revised run-time library with a windowing interface that is more platform independent than the AWT. In practical terms, part of the AWT has been replaced by a new set of classes known as **Swing classes**. These are incorporated into the current version of this course.

Example 2.1

In the object-oriented approach, identifying classes of objects and the relationships between these classes forms an important way of modelling the architecture of a software system during analysis and design. Using such class models provides the so-called 'seamless' approach to software development, which avoids the necessity of changing the type of model as the development process moves from analysis through design, implementation, testing and maintenance.

As you will see in more detail in Blocks 4 and 5, analysis involves identifying the classes that are important to the domain of the application (we shall refer to these as the application classes). Design is aimed at providing more detail on how the application classes are to be constructed and, in particular, on the components (classes from packages, in the case of Java) that can be used in their construction.

The specification of the human–computer interaction (HCI) part of the system is also undertaken during the design phase. A good design will attempt to separate the application classes from those needed to implement the user interaction.

In anticipation of the work on analysis and design you will be required to do in Blocks 4 and 5, a class diagram of the BallWorld program is shown in Figure 2.9.

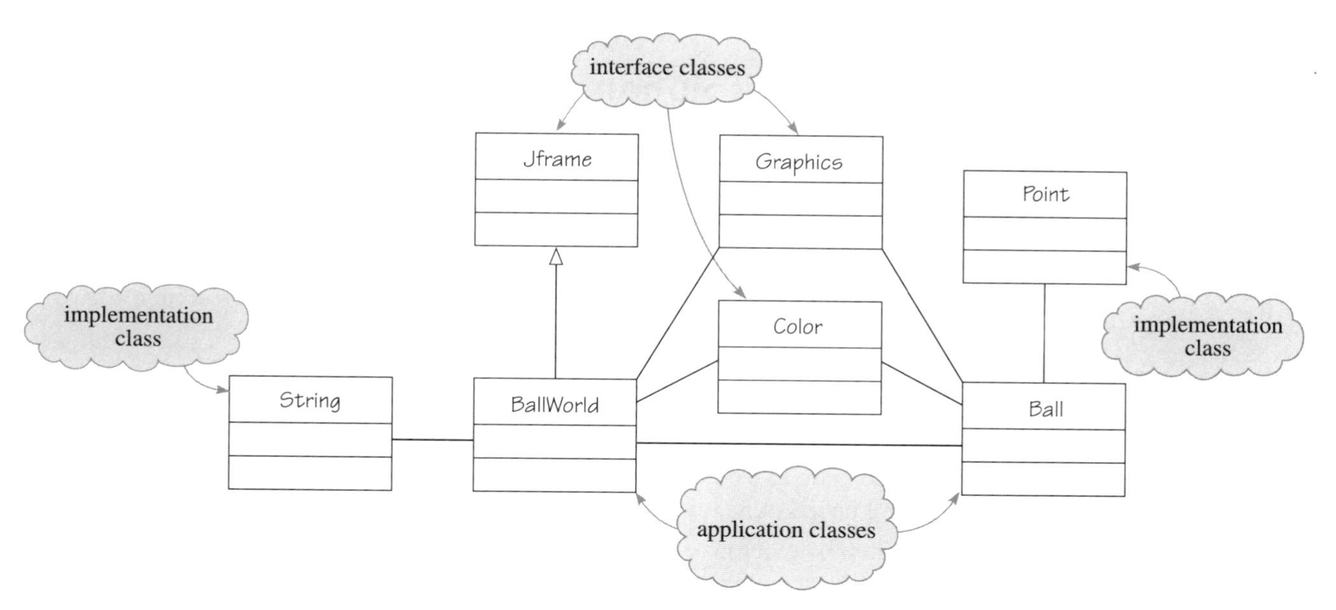

Figure 2.9 The class diagram for the BallWorld program

In Figure 2.9, there are two types of line joining the classes. The lines represent the two main types of relationship that can exist between the classes:

You will learn more about relationships between classes in Block 4.

- **generalization** (that is, inheritance) as indicated by the line with the triangle or large arrowhead which always points towards the parent class. For example, BallWorld inherits from JFrame;
- **association** which involves one class having one or more variables of the other class in it, either as data fields or as arguments in its methods. For example, BallWorld is associated with Graphics because of the use of the Graphics argument g in its paint method, and it is also associated with Ball because it has the instance variable aBall.

Classes can be partitioned into three groups normally known as application classes, implementation classes and interface classes. Figure 2.9 indicates which of the BallWorld classes fall into each category. Ball is an application class because it is central to the purpose of the application; Point, Graphics and String are implementation classes because they are used solely in the implementation of application classes; and JFrame is used in the design and implementation of the HCI part of the system and so is an interface class. While these classifications are not meant to be definitive, they do help you to think about the *process* of developing software (a topic that will be taken up in more detail in Blocks 4 and 5). In this example, it is difficult to classify the purpose of the class BallWorld. On the one hand, it serves to provide the windowing facilities that provide the user interaction; but on the other hand, it also accomplishes some of the movement of the ball, which could be considered an application-specific task. However, it is good practice to separate these two concerns as you will see later in PinBallGame.

It is sometimes useful to group some classes into a **package**, such as the Abstract Windowing Toolkit, AWT, which provides a range of related facilities.

2.4 SAQs and solutions

'Study Questions' are from Budd, Chapter 5.

SAQ 2.1

(a) What are the two ways to add Java source code into a project?

(b) What steps have to be taken in order to run an application once the source files have been entered into a project?

(c) How do you stop a running program?

Solution

(a) Java source code can be entered into a project either directly via the keyboard or by copying an existing Java source code file into the project.

(b) The first step is to compile the project (this can be done simply by clicking on the Run Project button). If errors are detected, the source file(s) must be edited to correct the errors. If there are no errors, the project will be executed automatically after you have selected a main class.

(c) A running program can be stopped by clicking on the Reset button that can be found in the bottom left-hand corner of the JBuilder window.

SAQ 5.1

(a) How would you change the colour of the ball in our example application to yellow? (Study Question 1)

(b) How would you change the size of the application window to 500 by 300 pixels? (Study Question 2)

(c) What does the modifier keyword **final** mean when applied in a data field declaration? (Study Question 3)

(d) Why do symbolic constants make it easier to read and maintain programs? (Study Question 4)

Solution

(a) The colour of the ball can be changed to yellow by changing line 5 of the program in Figure 5.2 to:

```
BallWorld world = new BallWorld (Color.yellow);
```

(b) By changing lines 11 and 12 of the same program to:

```
public static final int FrameWidth = 500;
public static final int FrameHeight = 300;
```

(c) The modifier **final** means that the variable cannot be modified, that is, it is a constant.

(d) Symbolic constants are useful because:

- they make it easier to change a program that uses the constant in many places – the final value of the constant only needs to be changed in one place;
- if an appropriate name is chosen, it will help to make the use of the constant more understandable to the reader.

SAQ 5.2

(a) What two actions are tied together by the concept of a constructor? (Study Question 5)

(b) What types of error does the use of constructors prevent? (Study Question 6)

Solution

(a) Object creation (bringing a new object into existence), and object initialization (initializing the data fields of the object, if any, to particular values).

(b) It prevents two types of errors:

- an object being created and used before it is initialized;
- an object being created and initialized several times before it is used.

SAQ 5.3

What does it mean to say that a new class inherits from an existing class? (Study Question 7)

Solution

In saying that class B inherits from class A, we mean that instances of B can access both the data fields and the methods of A (provided they have been defined as either **protected** or **public**). In other words, B inherits the functionality of A (but may have functionality additional to A).

SAQ 5.4

What methods inherited from class JFrame, are used in our example application? (Study Question 8)

Solution

```
setSize
setTitle
paint
repaint
show
```

SAQ 5.5

What abstraction does the Java library class Point represent? (Study Question 10)

Solution

The class Point represents a point in a two-dimensional plane whose position is located relative to a set of coordinate axes.

2.5 Exercises and solutions

[Remember to check whether an exercise from Budd, Chapter 5 is required for this year's TMA.]

Exercise 2.1 (Budd, Exercise 1)

The method Math.random returns a random floating-point value between 0 and 1.0. Using this method, modify the example program shown in Budd, Figure 5.2 so that the ball will initially move in a random direction.

Hint Look at the description of class Math in Budd, Section 17. 4 and see how a random number between 0 and 10 can be generated. However, to avoid reading a long description of the mathematical function named floor, simply multiply a random number obtained from the method Math.random by 10.0 to get a suitable value.

Solution

Introduce the following code immediately before line 20 in Figure 5.2:

```
double x = Math.random ()·10.0;
double y = Math.random ()·10.0;
```

Now change line 20 in Figure 5.2 to

```
aBall.setMotion (x, y);
```

The type of x and y has been chosen as double to match the types of the arguments of setMotion.

A better implementation that bypasses the need to create two new variables and simply involves altering line 20 is

```
aBall.setMotion (Math.random ()·10.0, Math.random ()·10.0);.
```

Exercise 2.2

Use the following Java code (which shows two classes that reference the class Ball as defined in Budd, Figure 5.3) to answer the questions that follow.

```
class TestBox {
   public static final int Xcoord = 10;

   static public void main (String [ ] args) {
      Ball b1 = new Ball (Point (Xcoord, 20), 5);
      Ball b2 = new Ball (Point (Xcoord, 10), 8);
      Box bx1 = new Box (1, b1);
      Box bx2 = new Box (2, b2);
      bx1.setNum (10);                                        // 1
      bx2.changeBall (bx1.getBall ());                        // 2
      System.out.println "Radius = " + bx2.getBall ().radius);
   }
}

class Box {
   protected int num ;
   protected Ball aBall;

   public Box (int n, Ball b) {
      num = n;
      aBall = b;
   }

   public int getNum () {return num;}

   public void setNum (int n) {num = n;}

   public void changeBall (Ball b) {aBall = b;}

   public Ball getBall () {return aBall;}
}
```

In the manner of *Unit 1.1*, Figure 3.3 and of explanatory note 3 of this section, draw the state of bx1 and bx2 (excluding the state of the ball)

(a) after the statement shown at the line marked //1 has been executed, and

(b) after the statement shown at the line marked //2 has been executed (you need not show the internal structure of Ball objects).

Solution

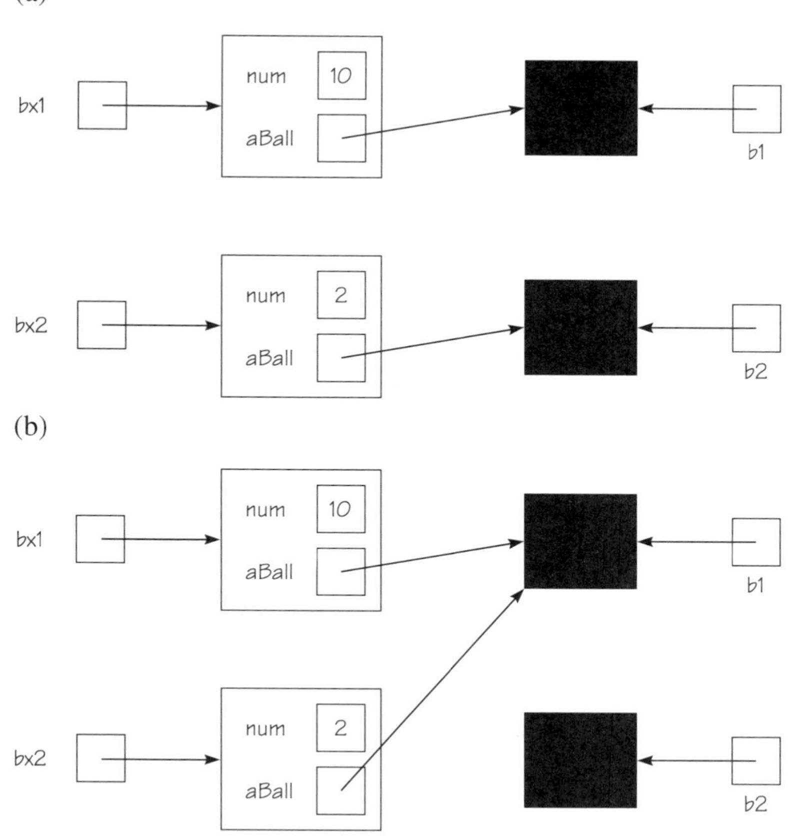

2.6 Summary of section

Read the summary in Budd, Section 5.7.

3 CANNON GAME: EVENTS, INNER CLASSES AND INTERFACES

In Sections 1 and 2 you studied programs that used the basic windowing facilities of Java. In this section you will learn more about these facilities and, in particular, how to use button and scroll bar user interface components also known as widgets. Widgets require an understanding of events and how to handle them when they occur.

3.1 Objectives

On completion of this section you should be able to:

1. understand the need for the 'wrapper' class Integer;
2. use inheritance to create a new class based on the Ball class introduced in Section 1;
3. use the pseudovariable `super`;
4. explain the use of inner classes and say why they are useful;
5. use interface classes and explain why they are useful;
6. describe Java's event model, involving events and listeners for events, and use buttons and scrollbars which rely on this model;
7. describe and use the default window layout manager;
8. write code which enables a window application in Java to be terminated by closing its window.

3.2 Key terms and concepts

The important terms and concepts associated with this section are as follows.

cast	graphical user interface (GUI)	override
command-line argument	inner class	radians
coordinate system	interface	`super`
event	interface component	widget
event-driven interface	layout manager	wrapper class
event listener	listener objects	
event model	`null`	

3.3 Study activities

By this stage it is important that you feel very familiar with the IDE, since using it to compile and run the *CannonGame* and *CannonWorld* programs will form a central part of your learning in this section.

1. Carry out the Practical Activities in Section 4 of the *IDE Handbook*, which involves importing, compiling and running the CannonGame program.
2. Read Budd, Chapter 6 up to the end of Section 6.1. You may find the explanatory notes below helpful in understanding some of the constructs used in the CannonGame program. Do not concern yourself too much with the geometrical intricacies of drawing the cannon; it is more important, at this stage, that you understand the use of the Java constructs involved.
3. Carry out Exercise 4.1 in Section 4 of the *IDE Handbook*, which involves importing, compiling and running the CannonWorld program.
4. Read Budd, Section 6.2.
5. At the end of each section of Budd, Chapter 6, attempt the relevant SAQ (labelled with the same number as the section of Budd).
6. Finally, when you have completed the above, attempt the exercises in Subsection 3.5 and check whether any other exercises from Budd, Chapter 6 are included in the TMA for this unit.

Explanatory notes

1 The value null (Budd, Figure 6.2)

The statement,

```
private Ball aBall = null;
```

introduces an instance variable, aBall, that will subsequently be used to refer to an object of type CannonBall. As this object has not yet been created, there is nothing for aBall to refer to. Initializing aBall to the value null is a way of indicating that this data field does not refer to an object. The value null can be used to test whether or not a data field refers to an object as is done in the if statement in the run method of Budd, Figure 6.2.

2 The modifier for class Cannon (Budd, Figure 6.3)

The fact that there are no modifiers preceding the class name Cannon means that, by default, the class is only accessible to other classes in the same package.

3 The class Integer and the primitive data type int (Budd, Figure 6.2)

As Budd says in Subsection 6.1.4, int is the name of a primitive data type but not the name of a class. Therefore, the operations of int are not represented by methods and are confined to the normal arithmetic operations such as add and multiply (the symbols, + and * represent int operations, not methods). If you want to use a value of type int where an object is expected, or want a method that manipulates integers (e.g. converts an integer to a string), you should use the class Integer. Instances of the class Integer are objects such that each Integer object contains (or 'wraps up') a data field of type int. The Integer class has a number of useful methods, one of which, valueOf, is used in CannonGame to convert a String object, args (previously read from the command line) into an Integer object. Subsequently, this object, referred to by the local argument theta, is transformed into an int value by the message theta.intValue () where intValue is another method of the class Integer.

There are more details of Integer and other wrapper classes in Budd, Section 19.1.

You can also convert a value of type int (such as 42) into an Integer object by writing,

```
Integer (42)
```

4 Radians (Budd, Figure 6.2)

See the *Glossary* for an explanation of this term and how it relates to angles specified in degrees.

5 Casts (Budd, Figure 6.3)

In the paint method of the class Cannon in Budd, Figure 6.3 there are the following expressions:

```
(int) (barrelLength * Math.sin (radianAngle))
(int) (barrelLength * Math.cos (radianAngle))
(int) (barrelWidth * Math.sin (radianAngle))
(int) (barrelWidth * Math.cos (radianAngle))
```

The construct (int) is known as a **cast**, and it is a mechanism for changing the type of a value, as we shall now explain. The value referred to by radianAngle is of type double (double precision floating point), so the values of Math.sin (radianAngle) and Math.cos (radianAngle) will also be double. This implies that the result of the complete expression (barrelLength * Math.sin (radianAngle)) will be of type double as will the result of the other similar expressions. However, the variables to which the values of these expressions are assigned, lv, lh, sh and sv, are all of type int. Normally, trying to assign a value of type double to a variable of type int would be an error. Placing the construct (int) in front of the double values is an indication to the Java system to convert the double value into an int. The system does this by ignoring the decimal part of the double and returning the integer part of the value.

It is not possible to cast any type into any other type; only certain type conversions are sensible. You will learn more about casts as the course progresses.

6 Drawing the cannon (Budd, Figure 6.3)

If you are interested in the geometry of drawing the cannon barrel in the method paint, the diagram in Figure 3.1, which shows the relationship between lv, lh, sv, and sh, might prove helpful. (Note that the paint method in Budd, Figure 6.3 uses the variable barrelWidth = 8 in drawing the cannon on the screen. In fact this variable should really be named barrelRadius. This is because the actual width of the cannon when it is drawn on screen, using the calculations in paint, is 16 and not 8).

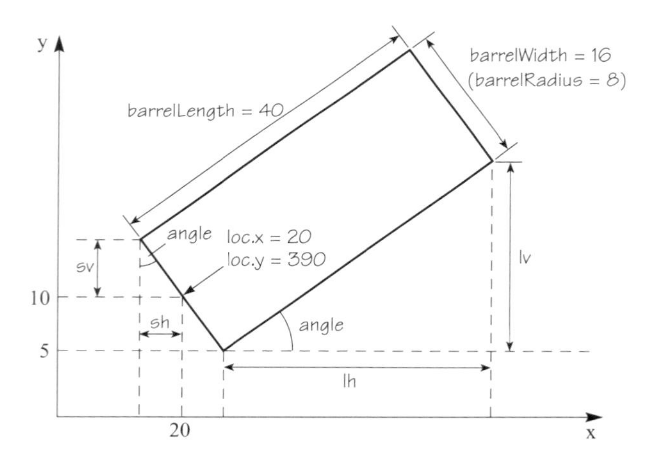

Figure 3.1 The geometry involved in drawing the cannon barrel

7 Imported packages (Budd, Figure 6.7)

In addition to the event interfaces, the AWT will also have to be imported with:

```
import java.awt. *;
```

and Swing also has to be imported with:

```
import java.swing.*.
```

8 Incomplete code (Budd, Figure 6.7)

Figure 6.7 is incomplete in several respects. Some code has been omitted from the CannonWorld constructor as indicated by the ellipsis. However, all the data fields shown in Figure 6.2 are also missing.

9 Inner classes (Budd, Subsection 6.2.2)

These are commonly used in Java to handle events. Java has three types of inner class, but, in this course, you will be introduced to two of them:

- member classes, for example, FireButtonListener and ScrollBarListener defined in Budd, Figure 6.7 where the inner class is defined at the same level as other members (data fields and methods) of the class;
- unnamed classes, which are defined within a creation expression. You will see an example of these when you study Budd, Subsection 10.5.3 in *Unit 1.5*.

In addition to data fields and methods, classes can also be members of a class.

10 Constructors for listener objects (Budd, Figure 6.7)

If you examine Budd, Figure 6.7 closely, you will see that constructors have not been defined for either of the two inner listener classes FireButtonListener and ScrollBarListener. However, in the body of the CannonWorld constructor there are the two **new** expressions:

new FireButtonListener () and new ScrollBarListener ()

which refer to default constructors. A **default constructor** is a constructor, already known to the Java system, which has no arguments, and will be used when a class is defined without its own constructor. Basically, the default constructor simply creates a new object of the class and does nothing more. (Refer back to SAQ 5.2 in Subsection 2.4 of this unit for a summary of the purpose of constructors.)

11 Events (Budd, Figure 6.7)

The event handling mechanism, illustrated in Budd, Figure 6.7, can be difficult to understand on first reading. Here is an overview of the process involving the fire button, which should help to clarify the issues for you (a similar process applies to the scroll bar).

- There are three activities associated with programming widgets: they have to be located at a chosen position in the window; they must be associated with a listener object (which detects when the widget has been used, that is, an event has occurred); and the action to be performed in response to the event (a mouse click, for example) must be specified.
- The action to be performed for a button, for example, must be implemented by a method named actionPerformed (declared in the ActionListener interface contained in the event handling package java.awt.event). This means that you must include, in the class that extends JFrame, an inner class, such as FireButtonListener, which implements ActionListener containing a definition for actionPerformed.
- The association of the widget object with a listener object is achieved by sending a message (such as addActionListener, in the case of a button) to the widget. This method passes the listener object (for example, an instance of FireButtonListener) as an argument to the widget.
- When fire is pressed by the user, the Java system automatically creates an event object of type ActionEvent, which contains useful information about the event (for example, the location of the mouse pointer when the mouse was clicked).

The above discussion illustrates why inner classes are useful. The method actionPerformed needs to access the private data fields (aBall, and cannon) of the CannonWorld class (these are not shown in Figure 6.7: see explanatory note 8, above). This is made easier by implementing FireButtonListener as an inner class. An ordinary class could have been used but this would have made the code more cumbersome and less clear.

The definition of the method actionPerformed (part of the interface ActionListener) includes a formal argument named e which must, therefore, appear in any implementation of the method. When actionPerformed is called, e will be assigned an object of type ActionEvent that will contain data about a specific event. In the current program, this information is not required, which is why e is never used inside the body of actionPerformed.

12 Inconsistent declarations (Budd, Figure 6.7)

This is an example of one of Java's **scope rules**: rules that determine in which parts of a program a variable or method can be accessed (referred to).

You may have spotted that the variable scrollbar is declared as an instance variable of the class CannonWorld, but the variable fire is declared as a local variable of the CannonWorld constructor. However, they both refer to widgets that are to be painted on the screen. There is no apparent difference between the roles of the two widgets, so why have they been treated differently? Certainly both could have been declared as private instance variables. However, both could not have been declared as local variables within the constructor because scrollbar is also accessed in ScrollBarListener (local variables can be accessed only within the method in which they are declared).

7 Read the second section of the *Case Study* entitled *Implementing a collection*, which contains examples of the use of constructors, methods and declarations.

8 Examine the classes Customer and BalanceHistory given in the third section of the *Case Study* entitled *An Example of Inheritance*, which contain examples of the use of accessor methods and arrays, as well as simple programming idioms that include determining the average of a set of numbers and finding the maximum value held in an array. There is no requirement to study this section in detail at this stage: use it as a source of further examples of the Java constructs introduced in this unit.

3.4 SAQs and solutions

'Study Questions' are taken from Budd, Chapter 6.

SAQ 6.1

(a) What is the parent class for the class CannonGame? (Study Question 1)

(b) In the first cannon game, how is the angle of the cannon determined? (Study Question 2)

(c) What is the difference in behaviour between a Ball and a Cannonball? (Study Question 3)

(d) How is the pseudovariable **super** used in a method? What effect does it have in a message expression? (Study Question 4)

Solution

(a) JFrame, since the class CannonGame extends (inherits from) JFrame.

(b) It is determined by using a command-line argument; for example, 65. This will be picked up by the method main as a string in args [ ], the first element of its array argument. The string object is converted to an Integer object using the method valueOf () from the Integer wrapper class.

(c) The behaviour of CannonBall includes a gravitational effect, which changes the motion of a cannon ball in the *y*-direction. In other words, the Ball method move is overridden in CannonBall.

(d) **super** is used in two different ways:

- as a method call in a constructor to indicate that the constructor for the parent class should be invoked using the argument(s) shown, if any;
- as a pseudovariable in a method to indicate that the method whose name follows **super** is a method from the superclass.

When a method in a subclass has the same name as a method in a superclass the subclass method is said to override the method in the superclass. The class Ball has a method named move, which is overridden in the subclass CannonBall.

SAQ 6.2

(a) What is an inner class? (Study Question 7)

(b) What is an interface? (Study Question 8)

(c) What would an interface for the class CannonBall look like (ignore the fact that CannonBall extends Ball)? (Study Question 9)

(d) What does it mean to say that a class implements an interface? (Study Question 10)

(e) What does it mean to say that a program is event-driven? (Study Question 11)

(f) What is an event listener? (Study Question 12)

(g) What is a window layout manager? (Study Question 13)

(h) What is the difference between implementing an interface and extending a class?

(i) Explain the use of the following method invocation shown in Budd, Subsection 6.2.5:

```
add ("North", fire);
```

Solution

(a) An inner class is a class that is declared inside another class. It is allowed to access the data fields and invoke the methods of the 'outer' class.

(b) An interface is similar to a class except that:

- its methods are not implemented;
- it is not allowed to have data fields except those that are declared **static**.

(c) The interface for the class CannonBall would be similar to:

```
interface CannonBall {
    public static final double GravityEffect = 0.3;
    public void move ();
}
```

Note that the data field GravityEffect appears in the interface because it is a **static** field.

(d) A class (say, B) implements an interface (say, A) means that B must provide implementations for *all* the methods listed in A.

(e) Being *event-driven* means that a program is structured around the idea that it performs certain actions in response to a range of events (such as a user clicking a mouse).

(f) Many of the components of a graphical user interface are associated with the generation of events, such as the user clicking a button or sliding a scroll bar. Such components have listener objects that will carry out specific actions when the event associated with that component occurs. It is the application's responsibility to provide the appropriate action. This is achieved by implementing the interface of the relevant listener.

(g) A layout manager controls the placement of graphical components in a user interface. Java has a number of such managers that allow various levels of sophistication in locating components. For a JFrame object, the default layout manager is the border layout manager. This manager allows you to place components in five different locations of the window: North, South, East, West and, although not mentioned in Budd, Center.

Note that Java only recognizes the American English spelling of 'center'. The use of 'centre' will cause an error.

(h) When a class B extends another class A, it means that B inherits not only the methods and data fields of A but also the implementations of A's methods. B might, of course, override some of the methods but ideally the purpose of the methods should stay the same, that is, they should achieve the same objectives. (It would not seem sensible, for example, to override a method whose purpose was to move a ball object with a method that printed out the colour of the ball.) In the case where B implements A, there is no implementation of A's methods to inherit, and so B must provide implementations of all A's methods.

(i) The method add comes from the class JFrame, the parent of class CannonWorld, that is, it is inherited from JFrame. In the given example, add uses the default layout manager to place the button referred to by fire into the "North" part of the application frame. Add is a message sent to the object to which the constructor CannonWorld () is applied, namely world.

3.5 Exercises and solutions

[Remember to check whether an exercise from Budd, Chapter 6 is required for this year's TMA.]

Exercise 3.1

Draw a class diagram of the CannonGame classes in a manner similar to that shown in Subsection 2.3, Example 2.1 of this unit. Distinguish between those components that can be labelled interface, application and implementation. The term 'interface' here is meant to refer to the classes providing the interface facilities for the user (i.e. user interface), and not to the classes referred to as 'interfaces' in Java. Similarly the term 'implementation' is meant to refer to those classes which provide the functionality required by the application, and not the class which implements a Java interface class.

Ignore the class Math and the awt classes Point, Graphics and Color.

Solution

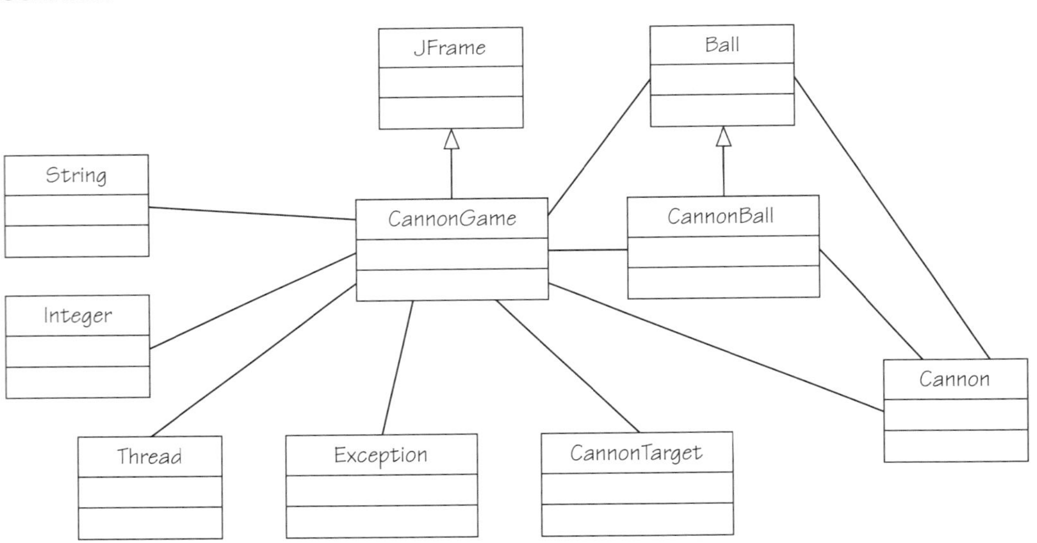

Figure 3.2

The application classes are: CannonGame, Cannon, CannonTarget, CannonBall and Ball.

The interface classes is: JFrame.

The implementation classes are: String, Integer, Thread and Exception.

The CannonGame class contains elements of both application and interface activities. A good design would separate these elements.

Exercise 3.2 (Budd, Chapter 6, Exercise 1)

Change the CannonGame so that the message being displayed provides not only the angle of the cannon, but also the current position of the cannon ball. This value should change as the cannon ball moves through the air across the screen.

Solution

In order to output the current position of the cannon ball, the paint method in the CannonGame class should be modified in such a way that, whenever the position of the cannon ball is updated, the printed message is updated and displayed. Here is our solution, which shows the additional statement in context:

```
public void paint (Graphics g) {
   super.paint (g);
   cannon.paint (g);
   target.paint (g);
   if (aBall != null) aBall.paint (g);
   String message2 = message + " Position = " + aBall.location ().x + ", " +
aBall.location ().y;
  g.drawString(message2, FrameWidth/2, FrameHeight/2);
}
```

Exercise 3.3 (Budd, Chapter 6, Exercise 4)

On some platforms it may be difficult to halt the cannon application once it has finished. Add a button labelled 'Quit' to the bottom (south) part of the application window. When pressed, this button should execute the method System.exit (0).

Solution

Here is a simple solution. Unfortunately, it results in the new button obscuring the cannon and the target. To overcome this problem requires some redesign of the CannonWorld class, but we shall not pursue this matter here.

The first task is to add a new button object to the window, which requires the following addition to the CannonWorld constructor.

```
Button quit = new JButton ("quit");
quit.addActionListener (new QuitButtonListener ());
getContentPane ().add ("South", quit);
```

Second, an additional inner class, QuitButtonListener, must be added to the CannonWorld class to specify the action that should be performed when the quit button is pressed:

```
private class QuitButtonListener implements ActionListener {
   public void actionPerformed (ActionEvent e) {
      System.exit (0);
   }
}
```

3.6 Summary of section

Read the summary in Budd, Chapter 6, Section 6.3.

4 SUMMARY OF THE UNIT

In this unit you have extended your knowledge of Java constructs by learning more about the AWT and Swing packages. You have also been introduced to inner classes, the use of interfaces, and learned more about inheritance.

You learned about Java's event model, used some new graphical components (JButton and JScrollBar), and you were introduced to the idea of a layout manager.

Unit 1.3 Using Inheritance

CONTENTS

STUDY GUIDE

Aims

The aims of this unit are to:

- reinforce the concepts of inheritance and interfaces;
- show how to capture and deal with exceptions;

Materials required

For this unit you will require:

1. this course text;
2. the *Glossary*;
3. the IDE;
4. the *IDE Handbook*;
5. the *Case Study*, Section 3
6. Budd, Chapters 7 and 8.

Required knowledge

You should have the knowledge and skills learned in *Units 1.1* and *1.2*.

Programme of work

There are two sections in this unit, and on the basis that an evening's work takes between 2½ and 3 hours, this unit should take you five evenings to complete (which includes answering the associated TMA question). An estimated study plan is given in the following table.

Section	Number of evenings	Materials required
1	3	course text; the IDE; *IDE Handbook*; Budd, Chapter 7
2	2	course text; the IDE; Budd, Chapter 8; the *Case* Study, Section 3

1 PINBALL GAME: COLLECTION CLASSES, MOUSE EVENTS, INHERITANCE AND POLYMORPHISM

In this section you will learn about:

- collection classes;
- handling mouse events;
- inheritance;
- polymorphism.

You will also learn more about the graphical user interface (GUI) facilities of Java.

1.1 Objectives

On completing this section you should be able to:

1. develop a program that will respond to mouse-related events;
2. use the `Vector` class collection class for holding objects and primitive data types;
3. describe what an *exception* is in Java and write simple exception handlers;
4. develop programs using inheritance and interfaces;
5. use polymorphism and polymorphic variables in your programs.

1.2 Key terms and concepts

The important terms and concepts associated with this section are as follows.

cast	mouse listener	`synchronized`
collection classes	polymorphism	`Vector`
exception	`sleep`	

1.3 Study activities

Since you will be required to run three versions of the `PinBallGame` program, this section will rely heavily on your ability to use the IDE. So if you have not already completed Sections 1–4 of the *IDE Handbook*, you should do so now.

1. Do Exercises 5.1 and 5.2 in Section 5 of the *IDE Handbook*
2. Read Budd, Chapter 7 up to the end of Section 7.2. Use the two programs — `PinBallGame1` and `PinBallGame2` — as appropriate, to support your learning of the constructs involved.
3. At the end of each section of Budd, Chapter 7, attempt the relevant SAQ (labelled with the same number as the section of Budd).
4. Do Exercise 5.3 in the *IDE Handbook*.
5. Read Budd, Section 7.3, using `PinBallGame3` to support your learning.
6. Finally, when you have completed the above, attempt the exercises in Subsection 1.5 below, and check whether any further exercises from Budd, Chapter 7 are included in the TMA for this unit.

Explanatory notes

1 The 'cannon' (Budd, Section 7.1)

You may be surprised that the pinball is defined as an extension of the cannon ball even though there is no cannon in the pinball game. This is because the behaviour of the pinball when set in motion is similar to that of a cannon ball. Balls begin their travels from a square box (described as the PinBallFire in Budd, Figure 7.3) at the bottom right-hand corner of the window (see the method mousePressed given in Subsection 7.1.2). They also respond to gravity just like cannon balls. Whenever the user clicks within this square, a ball is created at the mouse-cursor position. Subsequently, the ball's motion is controlled as described in Budd, Subsection 7.1.3.

2 The class PinBall (Budd, Figure 7.4)

The solitary **super** in the call super(loc, 8, –2 + Math.random (), –15) means that the method is inherited from a constructor in PinBall's parent class CannonBall (see Budd, Section 6.1.3). The relevant code is given by:

```
public CannonBall (Point loc, int r, double dx, double dy) {
        super (loc,r):
        setMotion (dx, dy)
}
```

There are, therefore two parts to this constructor: the first part (represented in the CannonBall constructor as super (loc,r)) is inherited from Ball and gives the initial location of the PinBall as loc and radius as 8; the second part sets the direction in which the pinball will initially move. The direction (dx = -2 + Math.random () and dy = -15) is predominantly north-westerly, but the use of the random method means that each new ball will move in a slightly different direction from that of its predecessors.

3 The symbols &, |, && and || (Budd, Figure 7.3)

The symbols & and | stand for the boolean operations 'and' and 'or' respectively. The symbols && and || represent variants of 'and' and 'or' known as 'logical and' and 'logical or' respectively. The boolean operations & and | have both operands evaluated before the operation is carried out. However, it is well known that the result of 'and' and 'or' can sometimes be deduced from the left-hand operand alone. For example, in the case of 'and', if the left-hand operand is false, the result must be false also, whatever the value of the right-hand operand. In the case of 'or', if the left-hand operand is true, the result must also be true regardless of the value of the right-hand operand. Therefore && and || have their left-hand operands evaluated first and, if the final result can be deduced, the right-hand operand is not evaluated. For this reason, && and || are often referred to as 'shortcut' operations and are particularly useful in constructing the conditional expressions used in **if** statements and in loops.

4 The **try** statement (Budd, Subsection 7.1.3)

Any code that can generate an exception should be placed in a **try** block (within the braces that follow the keyword **try**). A **try** block can be followed by zero, one or more **catch** clauses. Each **catch** clause specifies the type of exception it can catch and an exception handler. It is often the case that a fragment of code can generate more than one kind of exception, and hence there is a requirement to allow multiple **catch** clauses for a **try** block. The full form of the **try** statement is:

```
try {
   sequence-of-statements;
} catch (SomeException ex1) {
      sequence-of-exception-handling-statements;
} catch (AnotherException ex2) {
      sequence-of-exception-handling-statements;
}
    .
    .
   finally {
      sequence-of-statements;
```

```
}
```

where the optional **finally** block is executed when an exception that is not explicitly handled by one of the given **catch** clauses occurs. Java defines numerous kinds of exception but we shall be concerned with only a few of them in this course.

5 The variable world is static (Budd, Subsection 7.2.1)

In Budd, Figure 7.9, the implementation of the method hitBy consists of the single message:

```
PinBallGame.world.addScore (value);
```

The method addScore is a member of the class PinBallGame (see Budd, Figure 7.10). Since world is a **public static** variable defined in the class PinBallGame (see Budd, Figure 7.2) it can be referred to in other classes by the construction:

```
PinBallGame.world
```

Any **static** variable (provided it has been declared **public**) can be referred to in other classes by prefixing it with its class name. You have met a similar construction in Budd, Chapter 4:

```
System.out.println
```

where out is a **static** variable of the class System.

6 The spring (Budd, Figure 7.6)

In this example, a spring mimics the behaviour of a typical real-life pinball target which, when hit, gives the ball a slight ‘push’, that is, a small increase in velocity.

7 Different methods named intersects (Budd, Figure 7.6)

In Budd, Figure 7.6, a method named intersects is defined as follows.

```
public boolean intersects (PinBall aBall)
  { return pad.intersects (aBall.box ()); }
```

The method invoked by pad.intersects(aBall.box ()) is a *different* method from the one being defined. Since pad is of type Rectangle, pad.intersects(a Ball.box ()) involves a member of the Rectangle class. The method being defined in Budd, Figure 7.7 is a member of the class Spring.

8 What are the members of ScorePad? (Budd, Figure 7.9)

The fact that the ScorePad class has members named intersects and moveTo is not immediately obvious from its class definition shown in Budd, Figure 7.9. These members are inherited from Hole and Ball respectively.

9 Message sends without an explicit receiver object (Budd, Figure 7.11)

The condition of the while statement in the method hitBy is given simply by:

```
intersects (aBall)
```

This differs from the more usual message syntax in, for example, the line above it:

```
aBall.reflectHorz ( );
```

In this line there is an explicit receiver — aBall — of the reflectHorz message; in the intersects line there is no explicit receiver object. This is a shortcut: the message is, in fact, sent to the current Peg object. So that the interpretation of the line is: if aBall intersects the peg .... A slightly longer way of saying the same thing would be:

```
this.intersects (aBall)
```

In cases where there is no confusion, Java allows you to omit this.

10 Polymorphism (Budd, Figure 7.12)

The following code appears in method moveBalls in Figure 7.12 and is an example of the use of polymorphism.

```
for (int j = 0; j < targets.size (); j++) {
    PinBallTarget target = (PinBallTarget) targets.elementAt(j);        // 1
    if (target.intersects (theBall)) target.hitBy (theBall);           // 2
}
```

The variable target is used to hold objects of type PinBallTarget. Line //1, extracts an individual target from the vector targets and calls it target which is of type PinBallTarget but actually holds targets of type Hole, Peg, ScorePad and so on. Thus, since target can refer to objects of different types (though they must all be subtypes of PinBallTarget), target is said to be a polymorphic variable.

In line //2, the fact that target is a polymorphic variable means that the methods intersects and hitBy actually used are those that apply to whatever type of object target currently refers to. We shall have more to say about polymorphism in later units.

1.4 SAQs and solutions

'Study Questions' are from Budd, Chapter 7.

SAQ 7.1

(a) Why must the variable world be declared static? (Study Question 1)

(b) In what ways is a Vector object similar to an array? In what ways is it different? (Study Question 2)

(c) Given a vector people, which holds objects of class Person, write a sequence of Java statements which:

- places the size of the vector into the variable, total, of type int;
- adds the person, p10, to the vector;
- places the element at position 3 of the vector into a variable aPerson, of class Person.

(d) What is the relationship between MouseAdapter and MouseListener? In what ways are they different? (Study Question 4)

(e) What action is performed by the method System.exit? Under what circumstances in our program will this be called? (Study Question 6)

(f) What is an *exception* and how can it be caught and handled?

Solution

(a) The variable world is declared **static** in this case so that it will be available as a global variable to other classes that need access to the window object. (See also the solution to SAQ 4.5 in *Unit 1.1*.)

(b) Vectors and arrays are indexed collections. Unlike an array, a vector:

- can grow dynamically as new values are inserted into it;
- can hold objects (instances of classes) but not instances of primitive data types. You will see in Section 2, when learning about substitutability, that this means, in effect, that vectors can only hold objects of type Object because all classes inherit from Object.

(c) The code required is:

```
int total = people.size();
people.addElement (p10);
aPerson = (Person) people.elementAt(3);
```

Note the use of the Java expression (Person) in the last statement. This is a cast; it ensures that the object retrieved from position 3 of the vector is actually a Person.

Note that the position 3 of a vector is the fourth element of the vector. Like an array, the legal index values of a vector range from 0 to one less than the number of elements in the collection.

(d) MouseListener is the interface that lists the methods (or behaviour as Budd calls these methods) which are needed for responding to the different types of mouse-related event. Normally a class, which implements these methods, would be defined. However, in most applications, not all the methods are required. Therefore, to save programmers the trouble of writing unnecessary methods when implementing MouseListener, a class MouseAdapter has been predefined in Java. This implements MouseListener with methods that do nothing. Consequently, the programmer needs only to inherit from MouseAdapter and override those method(s) that are required.

The mouseClicked method assumes that the mouse is pressed and released quickly as part of one motion so that both events can be taken as being one event.

(e) The function System.exit (0) causes the program to terminate. This will happen in the case in question if an interrupt occurs while the Thread function sleep (which can throw an exception) is executing. There is a WindowListener interface, similar to MouseListener, which listens for the many actions that can be performed on a window. Not all of these will be required by every application so, as with MouseListener, Java supplies a default implementation called WindowAdapter that provides methods which do nothing.

(f) An *exception* is an error condition (or unforeseen event), which in Java can be caught and handled in such a way that a program can recover from the error systematically. Methods can be defined to 'throw' exceptions. Any code that can potentially throw an exception should be placed in a **try** block, which must be accompanied by a **catch** clause containing statements that implement whatever must be done when the exception occurs.

SAQ 7.2

(a) When should two software components be tied together through the use of inheritance rather than a common interface? (Study Question 7)

(b) What type of objects can by held by a variable declared using the interface PinBallTarget? (Study Question 8)

(c) How can inheritance and implementing an interface both be used when defining a new class? Give an example from the PinBall application.

(d) In what ways does the class Hole modify the behaviour inherited from class Ball? (Study Question 9)

(e) What is a Label? How is a label attached to a window? What methods are used to change the text of a label? (Study Question 10)

Solution

(a) Two software components should be 'tied together' through inheritance when one needs to share what Budd calls the *structure* of the other, that is, its data fields and methods, including the implementation of those methods. If, however, a component wishes to implement a type of behaviour that is common to many other components, but the implementation of which is specific to itself, then a common interface component, which all the components can implement, should be provided. In other words, *inheritance* should be used when there is a structural relationship between components, and *implementing an interface* should be used when there is what Budd calls a behavioural relationship.

Behaviour will be further discussed in Section 2 below.

(b) An interface can be used as a type. Consequently, a variable of type PinBallTarget can refer to any object that implements the PinBallTarget interface. For example, Wall and Hole.

Any variable declared to be of type PinBallTarget can reference objects of type Wall and Hole. Such a variable is said to be polymorphic.

(c) A class can both inherit (by extending another class) and, at the same time, implement an interface. The class Hole in Budd, Figure 7.8 is an example of such a class. Note that, although a class can extend only one other class, it may implement many interfaces, as shown in the following example taken from *Java in a Nutshell* (p. 79):

Flanagan, D. (1997) *Java in a Nutshell*, 2nd edn, USA, O'Reilly.

```
public class DrawableScalableRectangle extends DrawableRectangle
                                       implements Drawable, Scalable {
    // data fields and method definitions
}
```

in which the class DrawableScalableRectangle extends one class (DrawableRectangle) but implements two interfaces (Drawable and Scalable).

(d) The class Hole does not override any of the methods inherited from the class Ball. However, it does have additional functionality by implementing the methods hitBy and intersects from PinBallTarget. Note that Hole does not have to provide implementations for paint or moveTo because it inherits them from Ball.

(e) A label is a graphical component or widget into which text can be inserted using the method setText. In the case of the pinball program, it is attached to the window using the statement:

```
add ("North", scoreLabel);
```

in the constructor for the window.

To change the text in a label, use the method setText which takes a String argument.

SAQ 7.3

Budd, Figure 7.14 shows the MouseKeeper class. What is the purpose of each **if** statement in the method mousePressed? In particular, describe how you think the **switch** statement works.

Solution

Having established the *x*- and *y*-coordinates where the mouse was pressed, the first **if** clause checks whether the coordinates fall within the area for firing a pinball. If so, a new ball is added to balls and fired. If not, the second **if** clause checks whether the coordinates fall within any of the potential targets in the pallet on the left-hand side of the window. If they do, then depending on how many intervals of 40 pixels the *y*-coordinate represents (you will see from the code in PinBallGame3 that the potential targets are placed at 40-pixel intervals), the appropriate target will be created in the matching **case** clause of the **switch** statement.

The **switch** statement works by presenting a value at the beginning (in this case, y/40) which, if matched in any of the **case** clauses, invokes the statements in that clause. The **break** statement in each of these clauses is necessary in this example. This is because, once a case has been selected and the statements for that case executed, the **break** causes execution to continue at the statement following the closing brace of the **switch** statement (as required in this example). If the **break** statement had not been included then all the statements in the cases that follow would also have been executed. It is also possible to include a default case at the end, but in our example this is not necessary because if none of the targets have been chosen, element remains unassigned.

1.5 Exercises and solutions

[Remember to check whether an exercise from Budd, Chapter 7 is required for this year's TMA.]

Exercise 1.1

Draw a class diagram that involves only the target classes and the classes PinBall and Ball as defined in PinBallGame2 and PinBallGame3 on the course CD. Use the same notation for implementing an interface as used for inheritance. Using this diagram as an aid, explain how the method paint for the Peg class works. (Note that you are only required to show the inheritance lines between classes – you do not need to show any association lines.)

Solution

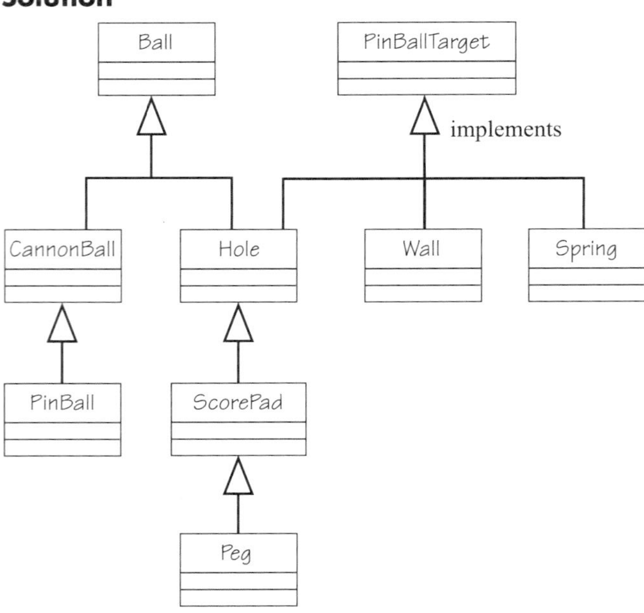

Figure 1.1 Class diagram showing PinBall and target classes

A peg is represented on the screen by two concentric circles. The inner circle is drawn by the paint method of ScorePad (via the message super.paint (g) within the paint method of Peg). The outer circle is drawn by the paint method of Peg either as a larger circle compared to the inner circle when state is 2 or a slightly enlarged circle otherwise.

If the peg has been hit, the class variable state in the Peg class is set by the hitBy method to 2. This means that the next time the peg is painted, an even larger circle will be painted (to simulate the peg responding to the hit). In fact, the repainting is repeated so quickly that it is hard to notice the peg responding in this way.

If a peg has *not* been hit, the class variable state in the Peg class remains 1. This means that the next time the peg is painted (which occurs when the method repaint is invoked in the run method of class PinBallGame) a circle is drawn, which is slightly bigger than the circle inherited from a ball. This is done by decreasing the x- and y-coordinates of the starting corner by $(r + 2)$ while increasing the width and height by $2^* (r + 2)$ where r is the radius inherited from Ball, making the circle bigger but with the same centre.

Exercise 1.2 (Exercise 5 in Budd, Chapter 7)

This exercise asks you to modify PinBallGame3. Budd in Section 7.3 does not describe this game in detail: he describes only the modifications that are needed to the MouseKeeper class. The important thing is that, in PinBallGame3, the preset targets used in PinBallGame2 have been replaced by a pallet of targets on the left-hand side of the screen (all stored in the targets vector). Note also that the pallet of targets is separated from the playing area by a wall, so that balls cannot strike targets in the pallet area.

In PinBallGame3, the items in the pallet are still stored in the targets vector, so that they will be checked for a hit, even though they can never be hit by a ball. A better solution would have been to create a new vector pallet that will hold these items, redrawing both the pallet and the targets on a repaint, but only if a target in the targets vector is hit by a ball. Modify the program in this fashion.

Solution

The required modifications are all to the class PinBallGame. First, a **private** data field is added to the class as follows:

```
private Vector pallet;
```

which is then created and initialized within the constructor for PinBallGame:

```
pallet = new Vector ();
pallet.addElement (new Hole (30, 100));
pallet.addElement (new Peg (30, 140, 100));
pallet.addElement (new Peg (30, 180, 200));
pallet.addElement (new ScorePad (30, 220, 100));
pallet.addElement (new ScorePad (30, 260, 200));
pallet.addElement (new Spring (15, 300));
pallet.addElement (new Wall (30, 340, 2, 15));
```

Note that the above code that adds the pallet targets to the pallet vector replaces the original code that adds the pallet targets to the target vector.

Second, in addition to the targets vector, the pallet is painted within the paint method of PinBallGame:

```
for (int k = 0; k < pallet.size (); k++) {
   PinBallTarget palletItem = (PinBallTarget) pallet.elementAt (k);
   palletItem.paint (g);
}
```

The actual targets will still be added to the vector targets and processed as before.

1.6 Summary of section

Read the summary in Budd, Section 7.4.

2 UNDERSTANDING INHERITANCE

In previous units you have seen how inheritance can be used to build classes based on other classes. This short section will clarify some of the important ways in which inheritance can be understood and used in Java.

2.1 Objectives

On completing this section you should be able to:

1 give an intuitive description of inheritance and the use of interfaces;
2 describe the methods of the class `Object` from which all Java classes inherit;
3 describe the concept of substitutability and use it as a programming mechanism;
4 describe the difference between a subtype and a subclass;
5 describe and use the forms of inheritance to which Budd refers under the headings of *specialization*, *specification* and *construction*.

2.2 Key terms and concepts

The important terms and concepts associated with this section are as follows.

abstract class	inheritance for specialization	`Object` class
inheritance as contraction	inheritance for specification	subclass
inheritance as extension	inheritance of code	substitutability
inheritance for construction	interface	subtype

2.3 Study activities

This section is about the basic principles of organizing a system using inheritance. Before you read Budd, we will review some fundamental principles of inheritance using examples you have already seen. This should help set the scene for the reading from Budd.

Inheritance and balls

The hierarchy of types of ball is given in the Figure 2.1.

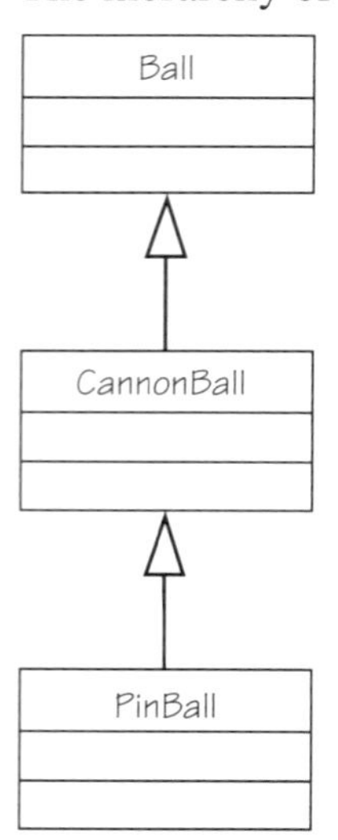

Figure 2.1 An inheritance hierarchy involving various types of ball

Pin balls inherit behaviour from cannon balls which, in turn, inherit behaviour from balls. However, CannonBall extends Ball's behaviour differently from the way PinBall extends CannonBall's behaviour. To understand this consider the original Ball class definition, part of which is given in Figure 2.2.

```
public class Ball{
   public Ball (Point lc, int r) {loc = lc; rad = r;}
   public void setColor (Color newColor) {color = newColor;}
   public void setMotion (double dx, double dy) {
      changeInX = dx; changeInY = dy;
   }
   public void moveTo (int x, int y) {loc.move(x,y);}
   public void move (){loc.translate((int)changeInX, (int)changeInY);}
   public void paint (Graphics g) {   // method to display ball
      g.setColor (color);
      g.fillOval (loc.x-rad, loc.y-rad, 2*rad, 2*rad);
   }
}
```

Figure 2.2 Part of the definition of the class Ball

Now consider the CannonBall class definition, given in Figure 2.3.

```
public class CannonBall extends Ball {
   public CannonBall (Point loc, int r, double dx, double dy) {
      super (loc, r);            // invokes Ball's constructor
      setMotion (dx, dy);
   }
   public double GravityEffect = 0.3;
   public void move () {
      changeInY += GravityEffect;  // this statement is short for
                                  // changeInY = changeInY + GravityEffect;
      super.move ();              // update the ball position
   }
}
```

Figure 2.3 Definition of the class CannonBall

All the methods of Ball are available to objects of class CannonBall. For example, if an object of class CannonBall receives a paint message, it will invoke the paint method from Ball. The difference between balls and cannon balls is in the way each moves. The move method as defined in CannonBall first changes the *y* translation — changeInY — by adding a gravitational effect, and then invokes Ball's move method: here referred to as super.move(). The move method has been overridden. The only difference between objects of class Ball and objects of class CannonBall is that they respond differently to these messages. There is no message that one can respond to and the other not. On the other hand, consider the definition of PinBall, given in Figure 2.4.

```
public class PinBall extends CannonBall {
   public PinBall (Point loc) {
      super (loc, 8, -2 + Math.random(), -15);
   }
   public Rectangle box () {
      int r = radius ();
      return new Rectangle (location ().x-r, location ().y-r, 2*r, 2*r);
   }
}
```

Figure 2.4 Definition of the PinBall class

Here, the constructor method is defined to allow for a small random effect. Moreover, a new method, box, is defined in PinBall to help detect whether a ball has encountered a target. If a box message is sent to an object of class CannonBall, an error will be reported; if a move message is received by an object of class PinBall, the move method from CannonBall will be invoked since that method has not been overridden in PinBall.

Inheritance and interfaces

The difference between implementing an interface and extending a class is subtle. Consider the definition of Hole, given in Figure 2.5.

```
public class Hole extends Ball implements PinBallTarget {

    public Hole (int x, int y) {
        super (new Point(x, y), 12);
        setColor (Color.black);
    }

    public boolean intersects (PinBall aBall) {
        int dx = aBall.location ().x – location ().x;
        int dy = aBall.location ().y – location ().y;
        int r = 2 * radius ();
        return (-r < dx) && (dx < r) && (-r < dy) && (dy < r);
    }

    public void hitBy (PinBall aBall) {
        aBall.moveTo (0, PinBallGame.FrameHeight + 30);
        aBall.setMotion (0, 0);
    }
}
```

Figure 2.5 Definition of the class Hole

The fact that Hole extends Ball means that, except where overridden, any method of Ball is available to objects of class Hole. For example, if an object of class Hole receives a paint message, it will invoke the paint method from Ball. That is, the methods mentioned in Ball do not have to be mentioned again in Hole, and if they are not explicitly mentioned the behaviour is inherited.

However, the fact that Hole implements PinBallTarget means that Hole.java needs to implement the methods hitBy and intersects that are part of the PinBallTarget interface. If it does not, the class Hole would not compile. Note that the other two methods that are part of the PinBallTarget interface, paint and moveTo, are already implemented because they are inherited from Ball. The point of the interface, PinBallTarget, is to specify what methods must be made available in any class that implements the interface. This allows you, for example, to define methods that can take an object of any of a number of different classes as an argument, as long as they implement the same interface.

1. Read Budd, Chapter 8 up to the end of Subsection 8.4.3.
2. At the end of each section of Budd, Chapter 8, attempt the relevant SAQ (labelled with the same number as the section of Budd).
3. Note that Budd refers back to chapters that you have not been asked to read. Nevertheless, the concepts discussed in those chapters should be familiar to you from your previous studies. However, if you wish to refresh your understanding of these concepts, you may find it helpful to skim through these early chapters now.
4. Finally, when you have completed the above, attempt the exercises in Subsection 2.5 below and check whether any further exercises from Budd, Chapter 8 are included in the TMA for this unit.
5. Read the third section of the *Case Study* entitled *An example of inheritance*, which contains an example of the use of inheritance and an abstract class.

2.4 SAQs and solutions

'Study Questions' are from Budd, Chapter 8.

SAQ 8.1

(a) What does Budd mean by the phrases, *inheritance of code* and *inheritance for specification*?

(b) Give an intuitive description of inheritance. (Study Question 1)

(c) What does it mean for a method to override an inherited method? (Study Question 2)

Solution

(a) By *inheritance of code*, Budd means the case where a class extends another class.
By *inheritance for specification*, Budd means the case where a class implements an interface. (But, as he discusses in Subsection 8.4.2, the same term is also used when a class extends an abstract class.)

(b) In programming languages, inheritance means the following.

- The relationship between the classes that inherit from each other is transitive. For example, this means that the class Peg inherits all the data fields and methods of ScorePad (since it extends ScorePad), but also inherits all the methods and data fields of Hole (since ScorePad inherits from Hole).
- The methods and data fields of a child class are an extension of the parent (i.e. they include the methods and data fields of the parent).
- The child class is also a contraction of the parent class, in the sense that it is more specialized.
- The two seemingly opposed concepts, *extension* and *contraction*, are easily reconciled if one realizes that *extension* applies at the class level and *contraction* at the object level. For example, consider the class Employee which inherits from the class Person. At the object level, there will be many more persons than employees since not all persons will be employees. In this sense, Employee is a contraction of Person. At the class level, employees will have all the methods and data fields associated with being a person, as well as those which are specialized to being an employee. In this sense, Employee is an extension of Person.

(c) If a class B overrides a method inherited from class A, it means that B redefines the way the method is implemented but keeps the signature the same.

SAQ 8.2

(a) What is the name of the root class for all objects in Java? (Study Question 3)

(b) What behaviour is provided by the root class in Java? (Study Question 4)

Solution

(a) The root class for all objects in Java is called Object .

(b) Object provides the methods, equals, getClass, hashCode and toString.

SAQ 8.3

(a) Explain why, if a class B extends a class A, an object of class B can be substituted for an object of class A. In these circumstances, could an object of class A be substituted for one of class B? Explain your answer.

(b) This is a modification of Study Question 5. Using the FireButtonListener and Button classes in CannonWorld (see Budd, Figure 6.7) as an example, what does it mean to say that child classes are substitutable for parent classes in Java?

(c) What is the difference between a subclass and a subtype? (Study Question 6)

(d) This is a modification of Study Question 7: using the classes Ball and CannonBall as an example, what are the characteristics of inheritance for specialization? Does inheritance for specialization support the subtyping relationship?

Solution

(a) An instance of B inherits all the methods and data fields of A. Therefore, if these methods can be invoked by an instance of A, they can be invoked by an instance of B. Hence, an instance of B is substitutable for an instance of A. (If one or more methods of A are overridden in B, an instance of B will still be considered substitutable for an instance of A.)

However, an instance of A is not substitutable for an instance of B, since it is likely that B will have more methods than A, and the additional methods would not be applicable to an instance of A.

(b) *Substitutability* means that an object, O1, the type of which is different from that of another object, O2, can under certain circumstances be substituted for O2. For example, in the CannonWorld program, the Button object fire, used to fire the cannon, expects to be associated with an ActionListener object. But ActionListener is an interface class and must be implemented. The inner class FireButtonListener in CannonWorld is the class that does this. It is a FireButtonListener object rather than an ActionListener object which is eventually associated with the fire button. But this is valid because a FireButtonListener object (the child) is substitutable for an ActionListener object (the parent).

(c) A *subtype*, as Budd says, explicitly recognizes the principle of substitutability. This means that a subtype object must behave in the same way as the supertype object, that is, it must respond to the same operations. So, for example, Employee is a subtype of a Person because employee objects behave like person objects as well as having their own specific operations.

In contrast, a *subclass* represents a way of creating a new class by extending another. Being a subclass does not guarantee that all the behaviour inherited from the parent class is sensible behaviour for the subclass. For example, it is perfectly possible to define Employee by extending the class Window, but doing so would be rather nonsensical because not all the behaviour of a window is sensible behaviour for an employee (see also solution (SAQ 8.4(c)) below).

(d) *Inheritance for specialization* involves the child class being a more specialized variety of the parent class, but satisfying the specifications of the parent behaviour in all relevant respects. The behaviour of a ball is in all respects appropriate to that of a cannon ball, and in this sense CannonBall is a subtype of Ball as well as a subclass of Ball. Note the fact that the move method of Ball has been overridden in CannonBall; this does not necessarily negate the subtyping relationship, but there are conditions that need to be fulfilled to ensure that this relationship is preserved. These principles will be discussed in Blocks 4 and 5.

SAQ 8.4

(a) What are the characteristics of inheritance for specification? How does this differ from inheritance for specialization? (Study Question 8)

(b) What is the difference between an abstract class and an interface? (Study Question 9)

(c) What are the characteristics of inheritance for construction? Why is construction not generally considered a good use of inheritance? (Study Question 10)

Solution

(a) The main characteristic of *inheritance for specification* is that it guarantees that the inheriting classes maintain a common interface, that is, they implement methods having the same headings. It is a form of inheritance for specialization except that the child class must provide the implementations.

(b) An *interface* provides no implementations for its methods and may only have static data fields. An *abstract class* is similar to an interface except that it may have methods that have implementations, in addition to those which do not. It may also have data fields that are instance variables. In the same way that it is not possible to declare instances of an interface, an abstract class must be extended and any abstract methods overridden before instances can be declared and created. In effect, abstract classes act like interfaces but may have instance variables and may also contain methods that are implemented.

Java is unusual in supporting interfaces and their inclusion in the language is a 'halfway house' between single inheritance (the ability to inherit from only one parent class at a time) and multiple inheritance (the ability to inherit from two or more classes simultaneously). Multiple inheritance raises a number of complex issues, which have been solved by some programming languages. However, we shall not pursue this matter further in this course.

A discussion of multiple inheritance, the issues and their resolution can be found in the book: Bertrand Meyer (1997) *Object-Oriented Software Construction*, Prentice Hall, ISBN 0 13 629155 4.

(c) *Inheritance for construction* represents the case where one class extends another in order to inherit *some* of the methods of the parent class. In other words, the two classes are not related as subtype and supertype, but they simply form a 'marriage of convenience'. This form of inheritance is *not* considered good practice because, even though the objects of the subclass will be substitutable for those of the superclass, it does not make sense to substitute one for the other.

2.5 Exercise and solution

[Remember to check whether an exercise from Budd, Chapter 8 is required for this year's TMA.]

Exercise 2.1

Modify PinBallGame3 in such a way that the class Spring overrides the Object method toString () to return a String object consisting of "Spring at" followed by the *x*- and *y*-coordinates of the position of the spring, for example, "Spring at (207, 194)". Furthermore, whenever a spring is placed on the pinball table the value returned by toString () should be painted above the spring.

Solution

Begin by adding the following definition to the class Spring:

```
public String toString () {
   return ("Spring at (" + pad.x + ", " + pad.y + ")");
}
```

Then add the following statement to the end of the paint method of the Spring class,

```
g.drawString (toString (), x, y);
```

2.6 Summary of section

Read the part of the summary in Budd, Section 8.9 that is appropriate to the parts of the chapter you have read.

3 SUMMARY OF THE UNIT

In this unit you have:

- seen how to trap and deal with methods that throw exceptions;
- learned in more detail some of the ways in which inheritance can be used, how it supports polymorphism, and how it contrasts with the interface mechanism;
- seen how new classes can be built from existing classes through the mechanism of inheritance, and that all classes in Java use inheritance;
- learned that inheritance is tied to the principle of substitutability;
- seen that inheritance can be used for a variety of purposes (not all of which are recommended in practice);
- seen how implementation differs from inheritance.

Reread the summaries to the Budd chapters that you have read in this unit; namely Budd, Sections 7.4 and 8.9.

Unit 1.4 Inheritance, Composition and Polymorphism

CONTENTS

STUDY GUIDE

Aims

The aims of this unit are to:

- study and use the Java mechanisms that support reuse, in particular, inheritance and composition;
- analyse some of the implications of polymorphism for an object-oriented language, such as Java;
- explore various forms of polymorphism.

Materials required

For this unit you will require:

1. this course text;
2. the *Glossary*;
3. Budd, Chapters 10, 11 and 12;
4. the *Case Study*, Section 4.

Required knowledge

You should have the knowledge and skills learned in *Units 1.1 – 1.3*.

Programme of work

There are three main sections to this unit, and on the basis that an evening's work takes between 2½ and 3 hours, this unit should take you five evenings to complete (including answering the associated TMA question). An estimated study plan is given in the following table.

Section	Number of evenings	Materials required
1	2	course text; Budd, Chapter 10, Sections 10.1 – 10.4
2	1½	course text; Budd, Chapter 11, Sections 11.1 – 11.5
3	1½	course text; Budd, Chapter 12 the *Case Study*, Section 4

1 JAVA MECHANISMS FOR SOFTWARE REUSE

This section introduces you to the two main mechanisms for building new classes from existing classes: inheritance and composition. It will also reinforce your understanding of substitutability and subtyping.

1.1 Objectives

On completing this section you should be able to:

1. compare and contrast the inheritance and composition mechanisms, and be able to analyse the main advantages and disadvantages of each in a particular situation;
2. use the knowledge gained by completing objective 1 as a guide to building classes using either inheritance or composition, or both;
3. describe how the *is-a* and *has-a* relationships relate to inheritance, subtyping and composition.

1.2 Key terms and concepts

The important terms and concepts associated with this section are as follows.

composition	*has-a* relationship	substitutability
data hiding	*is-a* relationship	subtype
encapsulation	reuse	

1.3 Study activities

You have already met many of the ideas to be covered in this section in *Units 1.1, 1.2* and *1.3*, but here they are looked at from the perspective of reuse.

1. Read Budd, Chapter 10 up to the end of Section 10.4.
2. You may be interested to skim through Budd, Section 10.5 to get a feel for what it is about, but a full knowledge of it is not required in this course.
3. At the end of each section of Budd, Chapter 10, attempt the relevant SAQ (labelled with the same number as the section of Budd).
4. Finally, when you have completed the above, attempt the exercises in Subsection 1.5 below and check whether any further exercises from Budd, Chapter 10 are included in the TMA for this unit.

Explanatory notes

1 The abstract data type stack (Budd, Section 10.2)

The abstract data type named stack, introduced in Budd, Subsection 10.2.1 is specified by the following four operations.

Operation	Action
empty	returns true if the given stack contains no elements, and returns false otherwise
push	returns the stack with a given element added to the top
peek	returns a copy of the element currently at the top of the given stack
pop	removes the top element from the given stack

Composition means implementing the class Stack in such a way that each instance of Stack contains a Vector object that holds the elements pushed on to the stack. The stack operations are then implemented in terms of the methods that are already defined for a vector object.

Inheritance means extending the implementation of Vector to include methods implementing the operations that are required for a stack.

In Subsection 10.2.2, Budd says that using inheritance provides more useful functionality than the version using composition because, for example, the Vector method size automatically applies to Stack objects. While it is certainly true that size may be a useful operation on Stack objects, it represents an operation that is not part of the specification of the original abstract data type stack which means that the inheritance version of Stack is not a true implementation of the abstract data type stack. You may well think this is a trivial point but, as you will discover in later parts of the course, writing programs that do not conform precisely to the given specification can be a source of error and can make maintenance a nightmare. More problematic than the size method, this inherited version will allow a user to remove items from arbitrary positions in the stack. This is very far from the spirit of a stack specification, and a system developer who expects a component to be built from a stack would probably assume that items can only be taken off the top. This could easily lead to erroneous behaviour. In Section 10.3, Budd gives several good additional reasons why inheritance must be used with great care.

2 Composition and inheritance in InputStream (Budd, Section 10.4)

Here is a concrete example of how composition and inheritance are used in InputStream. Figure 1.1 shows the FilterInputStream class inheriting from InputStream as well as having a data field of type InputStream.

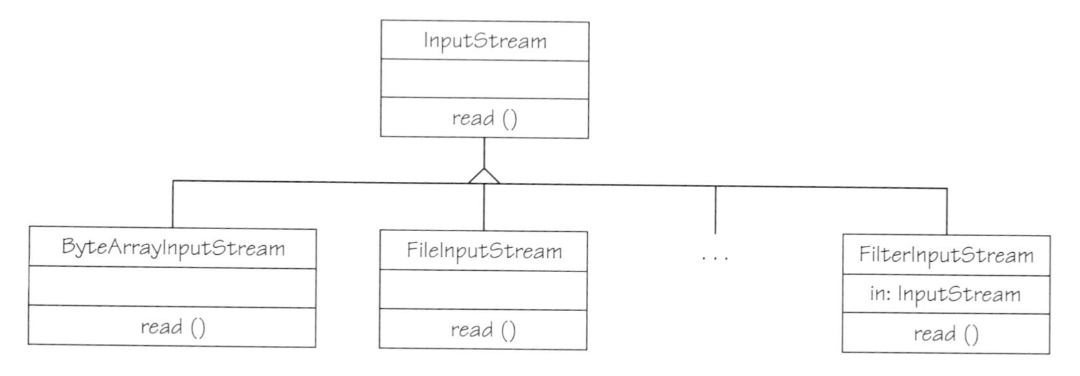

Figure 1.1 Inheritance and composition used by FilterInputStream class

Figure 1.1 shows that the class InputStream has a method named read, which is intended to return a single byte. This method is overridden in all its subclasses so that, in ByteArrayInputStream, the byte is taken from a ByteArray and in FileInputStream the byte comes from a File, and so on.

The new class FilterInputStream also overrides the read method but makes use of its data field in to provide a byte from whatever type of InputStream is referenced by in

```
public int read () {
   return in.read ();
}
```

Hence, whatever type of InputStream is referred to by in, this method will return a byte from that input stream via in.read () using the read method that is appropriate to that stream. For example, if in referenced a ByteArrayInputStream, the byte returned by the read method above would be from that ByteArrayInputStream. However, FilterInputStream also provides additional functionality. Suppose, for example, it were to count the number of bytes read via a new method named count.

This can be done by introducing a private data field number to store the number of bytes read and count will return the current value of number:

```
private int number;
public int count () {
  return number;
}
```

The read method defined above will have to be modified to increment number:

```
public int read () {
  number = number + 1;
  return in.read ();
}
```

To deal with the fact that there are several sorts of functionality that can be added to FilterInputStream, the Java library has been designed so that FilterInputStream has a number of subclasses, each of which adds a separate kind of functionality.

The term filter is normally used in contexts where each item of a data stream is processed in the same way. In the above example, each time a byte is read, number is incremented.

1.4 SAQs and solutions

All study questions are from Budd, Chapter 10.

SAQ 10.1

(a) Explain in your own words the principle of substitutability.(Study Question 1).

(b) When does the *is-a* relationship hold between objects, and what two mechanisms can be used to implement it in Java?

(c) When does the *has-a* relationship hold between objects and how can it be implemented in Java?

Solution

(a) The *principle of substitutability* states that there are situations in which one ought to be able to substitute instances of a child class where an instance of the parent class is expected. That is, a variable of one type is permitted to refer to an object of another type.

(b) The *is-a* relationship holds between two objects when the one is a more specialized instance of the other: that is, when the specialized object behaves in all respects like the more general object. This is similar to the forms of inheritance called *inheritance for specialization* and *inheritance for specification* that you met in Unit 1.3.

The *is-a* relationship can be implemented in two ways in Java:

- by implementing an interface, that is, when you wish to inherit a specification but not an implementation;
- by extending a class, that is, when you want to inherit the structure or code of that class.

(c) The *has-a* relationship holds when an object is composed of other objects, such as an aeroplane object has wing, engine, and landing gear objects. However, physical containment is not the only interpretation of *has-a*: a student having a tutor is another example of this relationship.

In Java, the *has-a* relationship is implemented by including, in the class defining the object, a data field of the same type as the component object.

SAQ 10.2

(a) What is meant by the term *composition*? Give an example.

(b) Budd says at the beginning of Section 10.2 that one way of thinking about inheritance is as a 'manifestation of the *is-a* rule'. Why might this statement need to be qualified?

(c) In Budd, Subsection 10.2.1, Stack is created from Vector using composition. Does this mean that a stack is substitutable for a vector? Explain your answer.

(d) How would you provide a size method for each of the Stack classes shown in Budd, Figures 10.1 and 10.2? Write code to implement it in each case.

Solution

(a) Composition means incorporating data field(s) into the definition of a class. For example, composition was involved in building the Ball class since it contains an instance variable (data field) called location of type Point. In other words, an object of type Ball is either partly composed or (*has-a*) Point object. The *has-a* relationship is often represented diagrammatically as a line drawn between classes as shown in Figure 1.2.

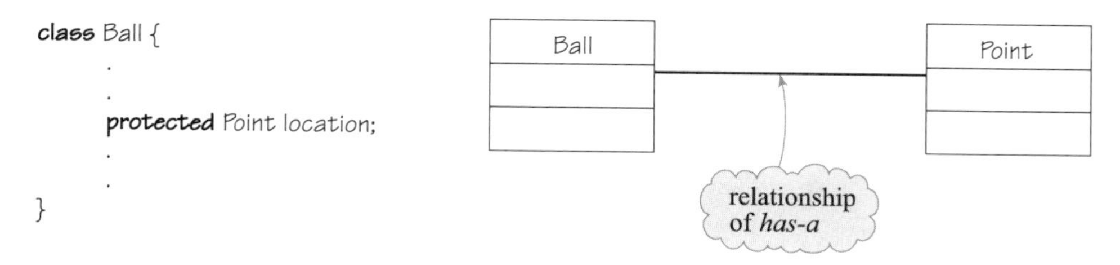

Figure 1.2 Class definition and diagram showing composition

(b) Inheritance can be a manifestation of the *is-a* rule, but only where the subclass is also a subtype. In the case of *inheritance for construction*, the *is-a* relationship does not exist (i.e. it is not manifested).

(c) No, a stack object is not substitutable for a vector object. Stack should not extend Vector because a stack object does not behave (have the same methods) as a vector. For example, there is no method enabling the user of a stack to find its size, as there is with a vector. Yes, Vector methods have been used to implement Stack methods, but not via inheritance, and therefore a stack does not behave like a vector.

(d) In the case of Stack that was built using composition, the size method would have to be implemented by writing a new method. For example:

```
public int size () {
    return theData.size ();
}
```

In the case of the Stack class built using inheritance (Budd, Figure 10.2), the size method is available from Vector without further effort because it is inherited. Therefore, no additional code needs to be written.

SAQ 10.3

Given the list of advantages and disadvantages of composition and inheritance in Budd, Section 10.3, how would you choose between them in practice?

Solution

If the class to be built is a subtype of an existing class, it is clearly advantageous to extend the existing class (that is, use inheritance). This is because, in our view, the advantages here (in particular, to be able to use substitutability, and not to have to repeat the definition of common behaviour) outweigh the disadvantages (to be able to see the state or data fields of the other class; that is, no encapsulation).

If, however, the proposed class cannot be considered to be a subtype of an existing class, that is, does not share the behaviour of that class (see the solution to SAQ 8.3(c) in *Unit 1.3*, Subsection 2.4), but still needs the behaviour of the other class in order to implement its own behaviour, composition should be used to build it. Here, the advantages (in particular, encapsulating the data fields of the component class) outweigh the disadvantages (e.g. not being able to use substitutability, which will be spurious in any case, and not inheriting some operations that may be useful).

SAQ 10.4

Draw a diagram showing the relationship(s) between the classes FilterInputStream and InputStream.

Solution

Figure 1.3 shows that FilterInputStream has a relationship of both inheritance and composition with InputStream. This reflects the fact that a filter input stream *is-a* input stream, but also *has-a* input stream.

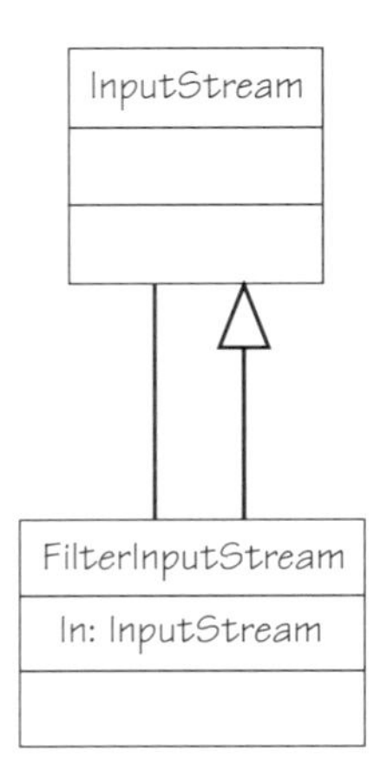

Figure 1.3 The relationships between FilterInputStream and InputStream

1.5 Exercises and solutions

[Remember to check whether an exercise from Budd, Chapter10 is required for this year's TMA.]

Exercise 1.1 (Exercise 1 in Budd, Chapter 10)

A set is simply an unorganized collection of values. Describe how you could use a Vector to implement a set. Would inheritance or composition be the more appropriate mechanism in this case?

Notes for this exercise

The Set class should provide the following public methods:

- addElement, which takes, as its only argument, an element of type Object and adds it to the set provided that the element is not already in the set.
- isIn, which takes, as its only argument, an element of type Object and returns the boolean value true if the element is in the set, and false otherwise.
- size, which returns an int giving the number of elements currently in the set.

You should also provide a constructor for the class. A full list of Vector operations can be found in Budd, Table 19.2.

Solution

Since a set is not a kind of vector, composition is the most appropriate mechanism to use.

```
class Set {
   private Vector theSet;

   public Set (){
      theSet = new Vector ();
   }

   public boolean isIn (Object anElement) {
      return theSet.contains (anElement);
   }

   public void addElement (Object anElement) {
      if (! theSet.contains (anElement))
         theSet.addElement (anElement);
   }

   public int size () {
      return theSet.size ();
   }
}
```

1.6 Summary of section

Read the summary in Budd, Section 10.6.

2 IMPLICATIONS OF INHERITANCE

Throughout this block you have been dealing with programs that use both inheritance and polymorphism.In this section, you will study some of the programming implications of using inheritance for the purposes of polymorphism.

2.1 Objectives

On completing this section you should be able to:

1. describe what is meant by a polymorphic variable and relate it to the concept of inheritance;
2. describe what is meant by, and exploit, the concepts of reference semantics and copy semantics as they affect assignment, tests for equality and copying objects.

2.2 Key terms and concepts

The important terms and concepts associated with this section are as follows.

activation record
actual argument
actual parameter
assignment
coercion
copy semantics
copying objects
deep copy
formal argument
formal parameter
heap
heap memory management
object identity
pointer
polymorphic variable
reference semantics
semantics
shallow copy
stack
stack frame
stack memory management
value semantics

2.3 Study activities

It is important that you feel confident about the concept of substitutability and appreciate under what circumstances it is permitted. If you are not sure, you may like to review SAQ 8.3(a) in *Unit 1.3*, Subsection 2.4 and Budd, Section 10.1.

1. Read Budd, Chapter 11 up to the end of Section 11.5.

   The details of Budd, Section 11.2 are useful but not essential to an understanding of the chapter as a whole. The explanatory notes labelled Stacks and heaps should be sufficient for our present purposes.

   Note that the opening pages of the chapter contain some new terminology whose definition will be given later in the chapter. However, this should not affect your understanding of the material.
2. At the end of each section of Budd, Chapter 11, attempt the relevant SAQ (labelled with the same number as the section of Budd).
3. Finally, when you have completed the above, attempt the exercises in Subsection 2.5 below and check whether any further exercises from Budd, Chapter 11 are included in the TMA for this unit.

Explanatory notes

1 Activation record (Budd, Section 11.2)

An **activation record** is also known as a **stack frame** and usually contains other information in addition to local variables (such as the place to return to once the method has completed its execution).

2 Stacks and heaps (Budd, Section 11.2)

The majority of instructions carried out by a computer when executing a program involves accessing data or other instructions in memory. Each item of data or instruction has an address where it is located. This implies that the address must be known before the data or instruction can be accessed. There are two fundamental occasions when an address can be calculated: compile time and execution time. If an address can be computed at compile time, it minimizes the time required to access the data when the program is running. We often say that such an address is **static** (it does not change at execution time) and *stack-based memory management* techniques are appropriate. If an address is not known until the program is executed, that is, the actual address has to be computed at execution time, clearly it will take longer to access the data. Such an address is said to be **dynamic** and *heap memory management* has to be used. For the fastest execution it would be preferable if all addresses were static. Unfortunately, this is not possible in general and, particularly, with polymorphic variables. Polymorphic variables can refer to objects that require different amounts of memory to hold them and it is not possible to know at compile time precisely which types of object will be referenced.

3 Method invocation (Budd, Section 11.5)

Whenever a method is invoked, storage space has to be set aside for its variables (local variables and arguments). When a method has completed its task, its storage is no longer required and the space can be reused by other methods. In general, a method consists of a sequence of calls to other methods. So, when one method invokes another the latter needs storage space but it cannot use the space reserved for the first method — because the first method is not finished. However, the second method will eventually finish and the first can resume. In general, of course, there can be a long sequence of methods invoking methods that themselves invoke other methods. The usual way to organize the storage space needed by each method invocation is to use a stack (a first-in-last-out structure). As each method is invoked, it uses the storage space at the top of the stack for its data. When a method finishes and its data is removed from the stack, the method that invoked it continues to execute and its data will then be at the top of the stack.

A non-polymorphic variable always refers to objects of a specific type and therefore its storage requirements can be determined at compile time. But this is not possible in the case of polymorphic variables since they can be associated with different types of object at run time, each of which can have different memory requirements.

2.4 SAQs and solutions

'Study Questions' are from Budd, Chapter 11.

SAQ 11.1

(a) What is a polymorphic variable? (Study Question 1)

Describe the connection between a polymorphic variable and substitutability.

(b) You are given the following class definitions:

```
class Shape {
    protected int x;
    protected int y;

    public Shape (int ix, int iy) { x = ix; y = iy; }

    public String describe ( ) { return "unknown shape";}
}
```

```
class Square extends Shape {
    protected int side;
    public Square (int ix, int iy, int is) {super(ix, iy); side = is; }
    public String describe ( ) { return "square with side "+ side; }
}
class Circle extends Shape {
    protected int radius;
    public Circle (int ix, int iy, int ir) {super(ix, iy); radius = ir; }
    public String describe ( ) { return "circle with radius "+ radius; }
}
```

Given the above class definitions, which of the following statements are legitimate in Java and why?

```
Shape s = new Square(6,8,3);            // 1
Circle c = new Square(10, 12, 4);       // 2
```

Solution

(a) A **polymorphic variable** is one that is declared as being of one type but may actually reference an object derived from another type. In Java, a variable derived from a class A is potentially polymorphic if A has subclasses. Polymorphic variables support substitutability.

(b) Statement // 1 is legitimate because Square is a subclass of Shape. This makes s a legitimate polymorphic variable in this case and it can reference objects of the subclasses of Shape.

Statement // 2 is not legitimate because Square does not extend Circle (that is, Square is not a subclass of Circle).

SAQ 11.2

(a) From the language implementation point of view, what are the two major categories of memory values? (Study Question 3)

(b) What is the solution to the conflict caused by polymorphic variables in regard to memory management?

Solution

(a) The two major categories are stack-based values and heap-based values.

(b) The solution to the problem of memory management caused by having polymorphic variables involves:

- not storing objects on the stack with their variables, but placing them in an area of memory called the heap;
- making the memory associated with the variable on the stack hold the address of the object on the heap; that is, 'refer' to the object.

Since references are normally represented by memory addresses that are of a known fixed size the compiler therefore knows how much space it has to allocate for the references. Thus, the problem is solved.

SAQ 11.3

(a) What does it mean to say that Java uses reference semantics for assignment of object values? (Study Question 5)

(b) Draw a figure similar to Budd, Figure 11.3 assuming that the following statements appear in the main method of the class BoxTest after the statement y.setValue (11).

```
Box z = new Box ();
z.setValue (9);
y = z;
x = z;
```

(c) What does the statement, 'Java uses *copy semantics* for assignment of variables of primitive data type', mean?

(d) This is a modification of Study Question 8: Using a ball object as defined by the Ball class in Budd, Figure 5.3. as an example show the difference between a deep and a shallow copy.

(e) This is a modification of Study Question 9: Using the call sneaky (x) in the main method shown in Budd, Subsection 11.3.2 as an example, show in what way passing a parameter is similar to assignment.

Solution

(a) The meaning of the word **semantics** is *meaning*! Hence, the term **reference semantics** is used when we wish to give a meaning to something in terms of references. Consequently, when it is said that Java uses reference semantics with regard to assignment, it means the following. An assignment statement involving two variables, say x = y, causes the reference (address) in x to be changed to the same value as the reference in y. In other words, x and y are made to refer to the same object.

(b) The three variables and the objects to which they point are shown in Figure 2.1. (We have changed the style of Budd's figure to show the state of the objects that have been created.) Notice that, after the operations in question, one object is not referenced by any variable. Budd, Section 11.5 tells you what happens to such objects.

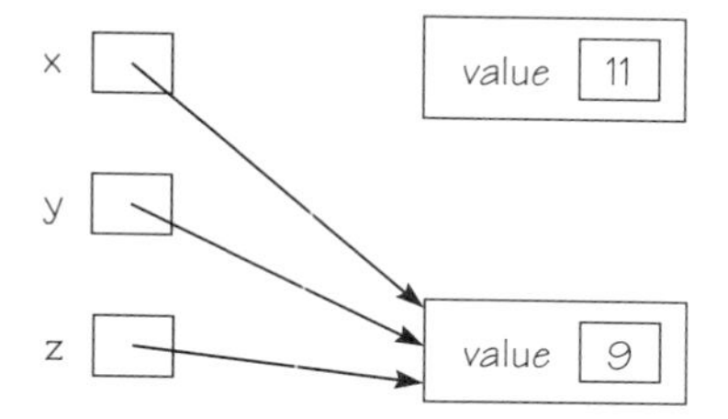

Figure 2.1 State of variables and objects

See *Unit 1.1*, Subsection 3.3 for further discussion on how objects and primitive data types are referenced.

(c) Variables of primitive data type store their values rather than references to these values. Consequently, after the assignment y = x (where both x and y are of type int and x holds the value 3), y would then hold the value 3; that is, a copy of the value held by x. This is known as assignment with **copy semantics**. To obtain the effect of copy semantics with variables that reference objects, another operation (not assignment) is necessary.

(d) A ball object is composed of two objects, a point referenced by loc and a colour referenced by color, and three values of the primitive data type: rad of type int, and changeInX and changeInY both of type double.

A shallow copy of a typical ball is shown in Figure 2.2, where both variables refer to the same point and color objects (since the loc and color variables were copied).

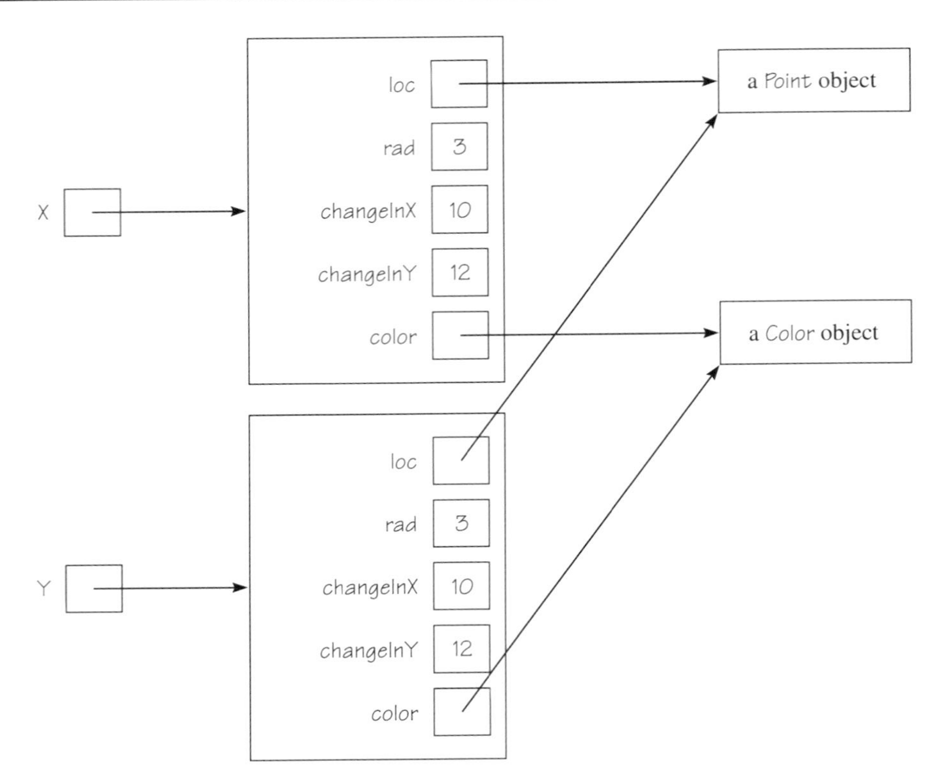

Figure 2.2 The object referenced by y is a shallow copy of the ball referenced by x

A deep copy is shown in Figure 2.3 where the Point and Color objects have been copied.

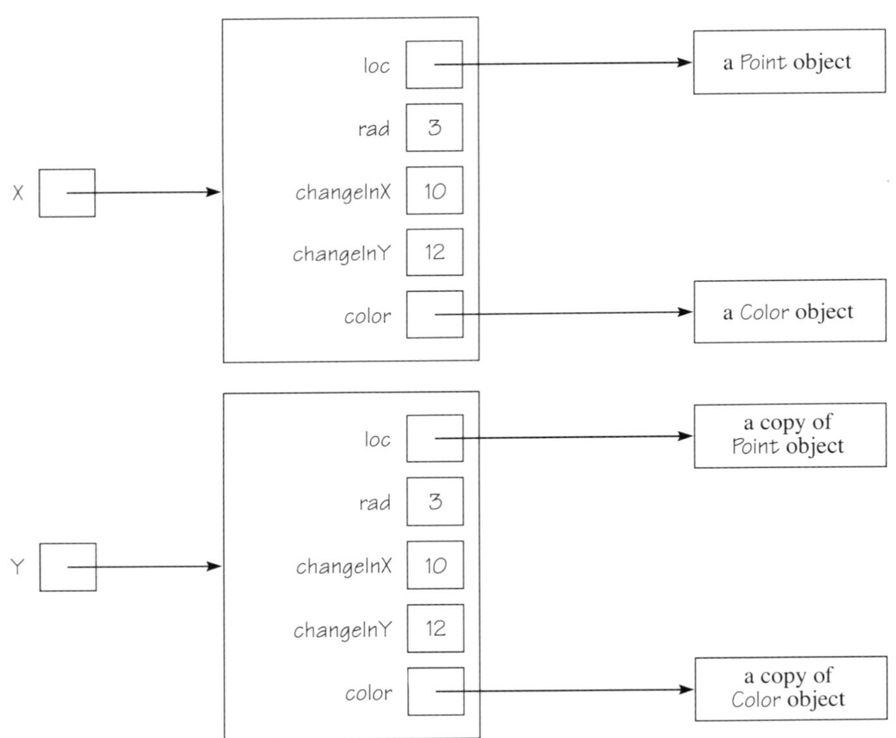

Figure 2.3 The object referenced by y is a deep copy of the object referenced by x

(e) The formal argument of the sneaky method is y of type Box. Notice that y is used as a local variable inside the method to set a new value for the box referenced by y. Now consider the call sneaky (x), where the actual argument x refers to a particular box object.Parameter passing, also known as argument passing, occurs when the object referenced by the actual parameter x is 'passed' to the formal parameter y. In other words, y is made to reference the same object as x. This is precisely equivalent to the assignment y = x.

SAQ 11.4

(a) What is the difference between the == operator and the `equals()` method? (Study Question 10)

(b) What complication, not mentioned by Budd, is there with the `equals` method?

Solution

(a) For objects the == operator (which is built into Java) tests for equality of object identity; that is, whether the two variables being compared refer to the same object. The `equals` method, in contrast, either inherited from `Object` or overridden, tests whether two separate objects are copies of each other, that is, have identical values in their data fields.

Figure 2.4 illustrates the difference between == and `equals`, where equals has been redefined for the objects in question. Figure 2.4(a) shows the only situation in which == is certain to be true, and Figure 2.4(b) shows a situation in which `equals` may be true (because the values of the fields in the two objects are the same (and == is definitely false).

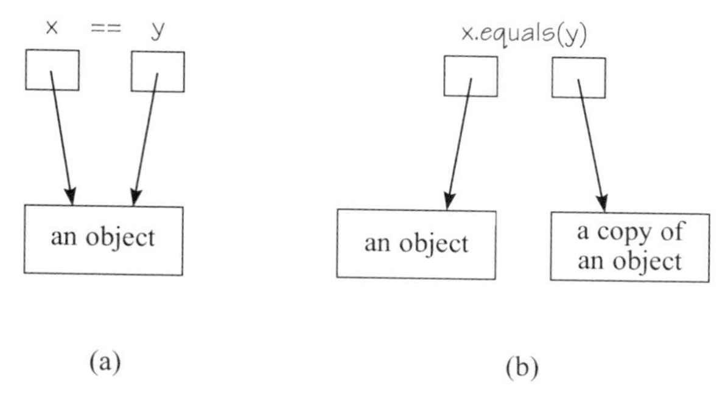

Figure 2.4 An illustration of equality object identity (==) and equality of object (`equals`)

(b) The complication with `equals` is that it needs to know whether the test is for a shallow or a deep copy. In practice, a developer when overriding `equals` would provide precisely the equality semantics required for the objects in question.

SAQ 11.5

(a) What task is being performed by the garbage collection system in the Java runtime library? (Study Question 11)

(b) What are some of the advantages of a language that uses garbage collection? What are some disadvantages? (Study Question 12)

Solution

(a) The garbage collector in Java recycles memory resources by periodically recovering the memory being used by objects on the heap that are no longer referenced by any variable in the program.

(b) A major advantage of having a garbage collector is that it saves the programmer having to write code that will do the task. Leaving garbage collection to the programmer can be a source of error because an object removed by the programmer might still have other references of which the programmer is unaware.

A major disadvantage is the degradation in performance caused by having to interrupt program execution while the garbage collector searches the memory looking for and removing unreferenced objects. However, as Budd says, the improvement in reliability is well worth the time overhead.

2.5 Exercise and solution

[Remember to check whether an exercise from Budd, Chapter11 is required for this year's TMA.]

Exercise 2.1 (Exercise 3 in Budd, Chapter 11)

Rewrite the class Box [given in SAQ 11.1] so that it supports the equals method. (The class Box is given at the beginning of Budd, Section 11.3.)

Solution

```
public class Box {
    private int value;
    public Box ();
    public void setValue ();
    public int getValue ();
    public boolean equals (Object arg) {
            // if arg references a Box object
        if (arg instanceof Box) {
                // assign it to a new variable
            Box argBox = (Box) arg;
                // check whether 'value' of current box equals the 'value' of input box
            if (this.value == argBox.value) {
                return true;
            }
        }
        return false;
    }
}
```

Note that:

1 The Java operator instanceof returns true if the object on the left-hand side (or more accurately, the object referenced by the variable on the left-hand side) is an object of the class on the right-hand side. If in this case arg does not reference a Box object, the method equals will go to the last statement in the method and return false.

2 If the data field value of the current box (given by this.value or simply value) is equal to value in the box input via the formal argument arg, the method equals will return true and exit. If not, it will continue to the last statement and return false.

2.6 Summary of section

Read the summary in Budd, Section 11.6.

3 POLYMORPHISM

Polymorphism, which means appearing in many forms, is a natural result of inheritance and occurs in a variety of guises. In this section you will study the various types of polymorphism.

3.1 Objectives

On completing this section you should be able to:

1. recognize pure polymorphism;
2. recognize overloading of method names;
3. describe the concept of coercion;
4. distinguish between overloading of method names in classes unrelated by inheritance and overloading of method names within the same class definition;
5. recognize parametric overloading;
6. recognize overriding and distinguish between replacement and refinement semantics;
7. understand the use of abstract methods;
8. appreciate why polymorphism may not be an efficient mechanism but provides other characteristics that are more useful to the programmer such as ease of development and use, and readability of code.

3.2 Key terms and concepts

The important terms and concepts associated with this section are as follows.

`abstract`	dynamic class	polymorphism
abstract method	overloading	pure polymorphism
coercion	overriding	refinement semantics
default constructor	overriding by refinement	replacement semantics
deferred method	overriding by replacement	static binding (methods)
dynamic binding (methods)	parametric overloading	static class

3.3 Study activities

You should have completed all the work in *Units 1.1 – 1.3* and the first two sections of *Unit 1.4*.

1. Read Budd, Chapter 12 up to the end of Section 12.7.
2. At the end of each section of Budd, Chapter 12, attempt the relevant SAQ (it is labelled with the same number as the section).
3. Finally, when you have completed the above, attempt the exercises in Subsection 3.5 and check whether any further exercises from Budd, Chapter 12 are included in the TMA for this unit.
4. Read Section 4 of the *Case Study*, which is entitled *The client program*. In that section you will see examples of polymorphism.

Explanatory notes

1 Static and dynamic binding of methods (Budd, Section 12.2)

For a typed language such as Java, when creating the executable (byte) code for a source code statement like aBall.move, it is, in principle, easy to identify the specific move method to be used: it is the one that occurs in the class to which aBall belongs. In other words, it is possible from a (static) consideration of the source, to determine which method is to be used, and to bind this method into the code before the execution of the program. This is called **static binding**.

However, in a programming language such as Java, which supports polymorphic variables combined with the overriding of inherited methods, it is not always possible to say, from a static consideration of the source, which particular method will be used when the program is executed. For example, consider the statement target.hitBy (theBall) in Budd, Figure 7.12. The variable, target, is of type PinBallTarget, but the actual object referenced by target at this point could be a Wall target, a Hole target, or any of the other targets that are defined as implementing PinBallTarget. Given that each of them has its own hitBy method, it is not possible to say until run time, when the actual object referenced by target is known, and which of the hitBy methods will be invoked. Consequently, the appropriate executing code can only be bound in (dynamically) at run time. This is referred to as **dynamic binding**.

In summary, languages such as Java that support polymorphism and overriding must also support dynamic binding.

2 The default constructor (Budd, Subsection 12.4.1)

The following paragraph attempts to clarify the last paragraph of Budd, Subsection 12.4.1, which is misleading in its reference to the default constructor and certainly does not tell the whole story about such constructors.

When **super** is used to call the parent constructor (as in the constructor for the DeckPile class), it must be the first statement executed. If no call on **super** is made explicitly, a parent constructor with no arguments (if one has been defined) will be called *by default*. If the parent contains no constructor with no arguments, Java will provide a *default constructor* with no arguments for the parent, and it will be this constructor that is called by default in the child constructor. If the parent defines a constructor with arguments, Java will NOT provide a default constructor, and the system will report an error if the child constructor fails to make an explicit call to **super**.

3.4 SAQs and solutions

'Study Questions' are from Budd, Chapter 12.

SAQ 12.1

What does the term *polymorphic* mean in common usage? (Study Question 1)

Solution

It means 'many forms'.

SAQ 12.2

(a) What is a polymorphic variable? (Study Question 2)

(b) How is the characterization of polymorphic variables different in dynamically typed languages than in statically typed languages? (Study Question 3)

Solution

(a) A *polymorphic variable* is one that can hold, or refer to, values of different types (i.e. subtypes of the type of the variable).

(b) In a dynamically typed language, *all* variables are potentially polymorphic since any variable can hold (or refer to) values of any type.

In a statically typed language, polymorphism is restricted to a variable being able to refer to objects of its class (i.e. its *static class*) and subclasses (i.e. its *dynamic class*).

SAQ 12.3

(a) What does it mean to say that a method name is overloaded? (Study Question 4)

(b) What does it mean to say that a value has been coerced to a different type? (Study Question 5)

(c) Describe two forms of overloading.

(d) What is parametric overloading? (Study Question 6)

Solution

(a) In Subsection 12.3.3, Budd refers to only two forms of method name overloading. However, elsewhere in Section 12.3, another form is described. Altogether there are the following three forms:

- where the method heading is the same as that in the parent class, but the body is redefined (this is the case of overriding ignored in Subsection 12.3.3);
- where methods in the same class (or classes related by inheritance) have the same names but different arguments;
- where methods in two or more classes not linked by inheritance have the same name (whether or not they have the same arguments is not an issue).

(b) *Coercion* occurs when a value of one type is converted to a value of another type.

(c) One form of overloading occurs when the same method name is found in two or more classes that are not related by inheritance. The second form occurs when two or more methods with the same name are found in the same class definition.

(d) *Parametric overloading* occurs when there are two or more methods in the same class definition with the same name but that differ in either (or both) the number of arguments or the type of arguments.

SAQ 12.4

(a) What is overriding, and how is it different from overloading? (Study Question 7)

(b) What is the difference between overriding using replacement and overriding using refinement? (Study Question 8)

(c) What is the default semantics for overriding for methods? (Study Question 9)

(d) What is the main characteristic of the default constructor?

Solution

(a) *Overriding* occurs when a method is defined in a class and a new method with the same name is defined in a subclass so that access to the method in the superclass is hidden. *Overloading* occurs when an identifier denotes more than one object (or method or operator). When a method is overridden, its name also refers to another method and hence overriding leads to overloading.

(b) *Overriding by replacement* (referred to as *replacement semantics*) occurs when the code of the method in the parent class is not executed (in effect, the code of the method in the superclass has been replaced by the code of the method in the subclass).

Overriding by refinement (referred to as *refinement semantics*) occurs when the code of subclass invokes the code of the superclass.

(c) Normally, overridden methods use replacement semantics. Constructors always use refinement semantics.

(d) The *default constructor* has no arguments.

SAQ 12.5

(a) What is an abstract method? (Study Question 10)

(b) What kind of methods are found in interfaces?

Solution

(a) An **abstract method** (also known as a **deferred method**) is a method that is specified in the parent class, that is, it is without a body, but must be implemented (i.e. the body must be defined) in a descendant class (e.g. the child class or a descendant of the child class).

(b) Interfaces contain abstract methods only.

SAQ 12.6

(a) How is an abstract method denoted? (Study Question 11)

(b) What characterizes pure polymorphism? (Study Question 12)

Solution

(a) An abstract method is denoted by including the keyword `abstract` in the heading of the method (and there should be no body associated with the method).

(b) The term **pure polymorphism** refers to situations where a method can be used with arguments of different type. This means that the formal arguments act like polymorphic variables (that is, the actual arguments can be subtypes of the formal argument). This means that the formal arguments (which are local variables) are polymorphic. That is, the actual arguments can be of different types, as long as they are subtypes of the type of the formal arguments.

SAQ 12.7

Why should a programmer not be overly concerned with the loss of efficiency due to the use of polymorphic programming techniques? (Study Question 13)

Solution

A programmer should not be overly concerned with the loss of efficiency due to the use of polymorphic programming techniques because they offer the possibility of rapid program development, consistent application behaviour, and code reuse.

3.5 Exercise and solution

[Remember to check whether an exercise from Budd, Chapter12 is required for this year's TMA.]

Exercise 3.1 (Budd, Chapter 12, Exercise 1)

Describe the various types of polymorphism found in the `PinBall Game` application presented in Chapter 7.

Solution

The `PinBallGame` program contains examples of all types of polymorphism. Here are some examples of each type.

Pure polymorphism

In the class `PinBallGame`, the variable `targets` is a polymorphic variable. The method `addElement` can take arguments of different type.

Overloading

The name `hitBy` is used for a method in class `Wall` and in class `Hole` (see Budd, Figures 7.7 and 7.8).

Overriding

The class Peg overrides the paint method (inherited from ScorePad).

The class MouseKeeper overrides the methods mousePressed and mouseReleased (inherited from MouseAdapter).

Deferred methods

The interface PinBallTarget specifies four deferred methods (intersects, moveTo, paint and hitBy).

3.6 Summary of section

In this section you have learned about various types of polymorphism and have been introduced to the notion of an abstract class.

Read the summary in Budd, Section 12.8.

4 SUMMARY OF THE UNIT

In this unit you have:

- analysed how the two object-oriented mechanisms of inheritance and composition can be used to create new classes from existing classes;
- learned why it is necessary, given the requirements of substitutability, for variables in an object-oriented language such as Java to refer to objects rather than store them directly;
- learned about the concepts of assignment and argument passing in Java;
- seen the need for different definitions of equality and copying resulting from Java's use of reference semantics for objects;
- learned about the different forms of polymorphism.

Reread the summaries in Budd: Sections 10.6, 11.6 and 12.8.

Unit 1.5 Swing, AWT and Applets

CONTENTS

STUDY GUIDE

Aims

The aims of this unit are to:

- investigate Java user-interface components, especially Swing components;
- introduce applets;
- study the classes for inputting and outputting data.

Materials required

For this unit you will require:

1. this course text;
2. the IDE;
3. the *IDE Handbook*;
4. Budd, Chapters 10.5.3, 13, 14 and 21.

Required knowledge

The learning acquired from *Units 1.1–1.4* is essential for completion of this unit.

Programme of work

There are two main sections in this unit. On the basis that an evening's work is between 2½ and 3 hours, this unit should take five evenings to complete. An estimated study plan is given in the following table.

Section	Number of evenings	Materials required
1	2	course text; the IDE; *IDE Handbook*; Budd, Chapter 13; Budd 10.5.3
2	1	course text; the IDE; *IDE Handbook*; Budd, Chapter 21
3	2	course text; the IDE; Budd, Chapter 14

1 SWING AND AWT PACKAGES

In the Java programs you have studied and extended so far in the course, extensive use has been made of the Swing package and, in particular, the JFrame, JButton, JLabel classes. This section, which is based on Budd, Chapter 13, aims to reinforce much of what you have already learned, as well as introducing you to a number of other useful Swing components. You will not be asked to cover them all but you may like to skim over those in Chapter 13 that are not included in the reading for this section.

The Abstract Windowing Toolkit (AWT) provides basic facilities for drawing graphics, e.g. drawing the lines and shapes as used in cannon and pinball worlds. AWT has been a core part of Java since the beginning, but Swing was only introduced with Java 2. Like the AWT, Swing provides GUI components — in fact they have similar names and functions (e.g. Frame is similar to JFrame and Button is similar to JButton). The main difference is that while the AWT components vary according to the underlying operating system, Swing components do not. For example, if you create an AWT button it will look like a Windows button on Windows based PC and a Macintosh button on a Macintosh. On the other hand, a Swing component will look the same on any platform. Swing is also larger and more comprehensive than AWT.

Given the superiority of Swing, you are not recommended to use AWT components in any Java 2 application. Unfortunately, at the time of writing, web browsers do not support Swing properly, so do not be surprised if your applets only work in the applet viewer that we provide you with.

Human–computer interaction is just one of the many terms used for the topic concerned with how humans interact with computers. Others include user interaction (UI), human–computer interface (also HCI), computer–human interface (CHI).

Although the topic of human–computer interaction (HCI) is not dealt with explicitly in this block (it will be dealt with in more detail in Blocks 4 and 5), the Swing package is clearly very much concerned with how the user will interact with an application. One of the aims of this section is to discuss some of the principles of HCI design and how the Swing package promotes these principles.

1.1 Objectives

On completing this section you should be able to:

1. explain the importance of HCI design;
2. describe some of the factors that contribute to successful HCI design;
3. use a layout manager;
4. understand the construction of, and extend, the Color Display case study which forms part of this section;
5. describe what is meant by an anonymous class;
6. include menus, text boxes and panels into your window applications;
7. construct a generic 'Quit' menu.

1.2 Key terms and concepts

The important terms and concepts associated with this section are as follows.

Abstract Windowing Toolkit
anonymous classes
BorderLayout manager
Color
Swing
Container
GridLayout manager
GUI builders
hash code (value)
hash function
human-computer interaction
JButton
JDialog
JFrame
JLabel
JMenuBar
JMenuItem
JPanel
JTextArea
JTextField
layout manager
this
unnamed class
usability guidelines
usability testing
Window

1.3 Study activities

Human–computer interaction design

HCI design is increasingly being recognized as one of the most important aspects of the development of a software system. You can build the fanciest and most sophisticated system in the world but if the users cannot interact with it easily, and enjoyably, all sorts of problems will arise; from disaster (caused by user error), and ineffective use, to not being used at all. In this sense, a system must be 'usable'.

The following factors are generally considered to constitute the 'pillars' of a successful HCI design.

1 *Guidelines for usability*, which take into account human factors like memory, problem solving, skill levels, personality variations, attention span, and psycho-motor skills.

2 *Prototypes*, which early in the development process provide users with experience of the 'look and feel' of the system.

3 *Usability testing*, which provides systematic and well-researched feedback on how the prototypes have been experienced by the users of a system.

See Schneiderman, B. (1992) *Designing the User Interface: Strategies for Effective Human–Computer Interaction*, 2nd edn, New York, Addison-Wesley.

A considerable number of effective usability guidelines have been drawn up, and many of these have been incorporated into standards that have guided the development of interfaces to operating systems such as Windows and Unix. You can browse through some of these guidelines by consulting the web page for this unit under the heading *HCI Usability Guidelines*. You will find that the guidelines are grouped under three headings.

1 *General interaction*, which includes:
   - being consistent, e.g. using a standard format and layout for menus, command input, and so on, throughout the system;
   - seeking efficiency in dialogue, motion and thought, e.g. minimizing keystrokes, the distance the mouse must travel, and so on;
   - providing help facilities that are context sensitive, e.g. those facilities that give the user access to topics that are relevant to the actions they are currently carrying out.

2 *Information display*, which includes:
   - displaying only the information that is relevant to the current context;
   - not overwhelming the user with data.

3 *Data input*, which includes:
   - minimizing the number of input actions required of the user, e.g. by using predefined selections for the user to choose from;
   - deactivating commands that are inappropriate in the context of current actions.

Java Swing provides the classes to build sophisticated user interfaces embodying the usability guidelines mentioned above. In fact, some of the usability guidelines have already been incorporated into the components provided by Swing. For example, all the components are designed to provide the same consistent look and feel as experienced throughout a Windows environment (which in turn is similar to the interfaces provided by other operating systems).

You have already seen how some of the Swing classes, such as the `CannonGame` and the `PinBallGame`, can be used to provide interfaces to applications. You will have found that creating components for the interface, such as windows, buttons and sliders, and providing event-based actions to use them was not a trivial task. However, many development environments (including the IDE used on this course) have facilities, often referred to as *GUI builders*, which make it much easier to create interfaces. This is achieved, for example, by providing a palette of components which can be 'dragged-and-dropped' using the mouse, by making it easy to link actions to events, and so on.

The next practical activity will give you some experience with using the GUI builder in the IDE.

1 Do the practical activity and exercise in Section 6 of the *IDE Handbook*.

Clearly, GUI builders similar to that in your IDE contribute to successful HCI development, in that they enable the developer to prototype interfaces rapidly. This in turn means that users can try out the system and provide feedback to the usability of the system.

The availability of prototypes early in the process of development also facilitates the more formal and systematic process of *usability testing*. This generally involves selected users undertaking carefully designed tasks so that measures of usability can be calculated and fed back into the development process.

2 Now attempt SAQ 1.1.

Swing facilities not yet encountered

In this subsection, you will continue your study of the Swing package.

First, ensure that you have done the exercise in Section 6 of the *IDE Handbook*, since it introduces the `ColorTest` application discussed by Budd. Make sure you understand what the program achieves, and how certain graphical user interface components are used. Second, you read the initial sections of Budd, Chapter 13 to learn more about Java Swing, in particular, the layout manager and its graphical user interface (GUI) components. You will then be in a position to understand the design of the `ColorTest` program. Third, you complete the study of Budd, Chapter 13 which examines dialog windows and the menu bar.

In Budd, Subsection 13.3.2 and the `ColorTest` application, class definition expressions involving anonymous classes are used. Therefore, you are advised to interrupt your study of Budd, Chapter 13 to study Budd, Chapter 10.5.3 where these ideas are explained.

3 Read Budd, Chapter 13, Sections 13.1–13.4.
4 Read Budd, Subsection 10.5.3, *Unnamed Classes*, since an example of such a class is used in the `ColorTest` Program.
5 Read Budd, Sections 13.5 and 13.7.
6 Read the explanatory notes, if any, associated with the relevant section.
7 At the end of each section of Budd, Chapter 13, attempt the relevant SAQ (labelled with the same number as the section of Budd).
8 Finally, when you have completed the above, attempt the exercises in Subsection 1.5 and check whether any further exercises from Budd, Chapter 13 are included in the TMA for this unit.

Explanatory notes

1 Hash code (Budd, Section 13.1)

A hash code (or hash value) is an integer that has been computed from the object. The algorithm for calculating the integer is called a **hash function** and is usually designed to be a fast computation. The hash value can be used in a program to identify the object. Unfortunately, the nature of hash values is that they are not guaranteed to be unique: two or more objects could have the same hash value.

2 Anonymous (unnamed) classes (Budd, Subsection 10.5.3)

Anonymous classes have a number of rules associated with them. First, if the name following **new** has the same name as an existing class, it is assumed that the anonymous class extends that class. For example, in the case of the anonymous class used in ColorTest (at the end of the method makeColorButtons) the name after **new** is ButtonAdapter, which is a name of a class in the program. This means that the anonymous class extends the ButtonAdapter class, and in the process implements the abstract method pressed.

Second, apart from the first rule, anonymous classes cannot be defined as either extending another class or implementing an interface.

3 The class BrightenButton (Budd, Section 13.5)

The following Java construct:

```
i == 0 ? "brighter" : "darker"
```

which appears as an argument to **super** has not been encountered before. It is a Java construct that means 'if i has the value 0 then return the string "brighter" as the argument to **super**; else return the string "darker" '. Since it is an expression that returns a value, it saves writing the following equivalent code using an **if** statement:

```
if (i == 0)
   super ("brighter")
else
   super ("darker");
```

1.4 SAQs and solutions

'Study Questions' are from Budd, Chapter 13.

SAQ 1.1

(a) Why is HCI design so important?

(b) Rank the three 'pillars' of a successful HCI design in order of importance.

(c) What is a GUI builder?

Solution

(a) HCI design is important because ultimately the success of a software system hangs or falls on whether the users are able to use it effectively and perhaps, more importantly, enjoyably and safely.

(b) This is a difficult question. In our view, there is a sense in which they stand or fall together. Guidelines are clearly useful, but are of limited value if the user has not had a chance to test out the system and has not been able to use the feedback to improve the system.

(c) A GUI builder is a tool incorporated into a programming development environment which enables interfaces (using components such as those provided by Java Swing) to be built quickly and easily; for example, using drag-and-drop techniques.

SAQ 13.1

(a) What is Component object in the Java AWT? (Study Question 2)

(b) What are the parent classes of class JFrame? (Study Question 3)

(c) In what class is the method setBackground defined? (Study Question 4)

(d) How is a container different from other kinds of components? (Study Question 5)

(e) Explain whether or not it is possible to nest a JTextArea object inside a JDialog object.

(f) What is the difference between a frame, a window, and a container? (Study Question 6)

(g) Explain why in a framework there are two views of an overridden method, such as paint. (Study Question 7)

Solution

(a) In Java, an object of class Component is an object that can be displayed on a two-dimensional screen and with which the user can interact.

(b) Parent of Jframe is Frame, parent of Frame is Window. Container is the parent of Window, Component is the parent of Container, and Object is the parent of Component.

(c) The method setBackground is defined in Component.

(d) A Container object is different from other types of components because it can nest (hold) other components within it. Such objects, that is, all the objects derived from the classes in the Container hierarchy, are used to develop complex graphical interfaces.

(e) Yes, this is possible because a JTextArea object *is-a* Component object, and a JDialog object *is-a* Container object that can nest Component objects such as a text area. The reverse is not true because a JTextArea object is not a Container object.

(f) A frame *is-a* window that can have a title bar, a menu bar, a border, a cursor, and so on, and hence it has methods, such as setTitle, setCursor, and setMenuBar.

- A window *is-a* container that can be displayed on an output device using the method show. Windows can be placed on top of one another so that they overlap on the screen. The methods toFront and toBack change the order in which windows are placed on each other and hence determine which window is on top.
- A container *is-a* component that can nest other components within it.

(g) When the method show in Window is called, it invokes a method setVisible in its parent class Component. This in turn invokes repaint and paint, which are also found in Component. In this view, it is the paint method from Component that is being executed. However, the other view is that the actual paint method that is invoked is the one which has been redefined in the application class.

SAQ 13.2

(a) What is the task performed by the layout manager? (Study Question 8)

(b) Explain how the three mechanisms of inheritance, composition, and implementation of an interface are all involved in the task of attaching a layout manager to a container. (Study Question 9)

(c) What is the difference between a BorderLayout and a GridLayout manager?

Solution

(a) The layout manager places in position the list of components held in a container.

(b) Inheritance allows the application class to use the setLayout method from Container, which enables an instance of the layout manager to be added to the application frame.

Composition is involved because the class Container *has-a* LayoutManager (i.e. a data field that references a particular layout manager).

Implementing an interface is required because the actual layout manager being used is an object of a class that implements the LayoutManager interface.

Note that polymorphism is used because the actual layout manager held by the frame is not an object of LayoutManager but an instance of one of its subclasses. In other words, the data field in the application frame referencing the layout manager is a polymorphic variable.

(c) A BorderLayout manager can only manage five different components positioned at the top, bottom, sides and centre of a JFrame object.

A GridLayout manager provides a layout that is a two-dimensional array of similar sized areas each of which can contain one component.

SAQ 13.3

In Subsection 13.3.2, Budd describes two different methods for creating a listener object and attaching it to a colour button. What is the difference between the two methods?

Solution

In the first method, the button and its listener are separate objects: the first is an instance of the class JButton and the second an instance of the class DoIt. The listener is added to the button using the Button method addActionListener.

The second method involves creating an object that is both a button (in this case, a colour button) and a listener. However, since a button expects a listener to be added to it (because the new button object will inherit a data field for a listener), it means that a button-listener (in its role as a listener) must be added to itself (in its role as a button)! This is achieved using the method call addActionListener (this) in the constructor for a button-listener, where this is a reference to the object on which the method addActionListener is executing (or, in the case where the method is a constructor, the object that is being created). Note that Budd takes the latter technique one step further and defines a general solution.

The second method may seem confusing at first sight. However, thinking in terms of objects and memory locations, all that is meant is that, in any button-listener object, the data field for the listener is made to refer to the button-listener itself, as shown in Figure 1.1.

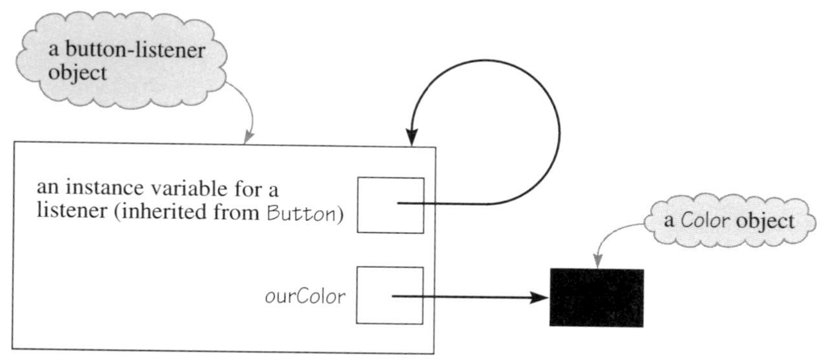

Figure 1.1 A button-listener object with a data field referring to itself

SAQ 13.4

What is a JPanel?(Study Question 15)

Solution

A JPanel is both a Container and a Component. It can hold its own layout manager for inserting components into it. Like any component, it must in turn be inserted into the application display.

SAQ 13.5

(a) How many components are held in the ColorTest window?

(b) What do the three numerical values that define a colour represent? (Study Question 17)

(c) In the ColorTest Program shown in Budd, Figure 13.12, explain the workings of the methods setFromBar and setFromColor. Where do they get invoked?

(d) Explain the use of the JPanel for colour buttons in the ColorTest program in terms of the layout managers with which it is involved.

Solution

(a) There are 23: the text field at the top (1); one panel with sixteen buttons (17); a second panel for the colour field (1); a third panel with three sliders (4).

(b) The constructor for class Color can take three integer arguments, which represent the saturation values for red, blue and green. The arguments must be integers between 0 and 255, where 0 represents no component of that colour and 255 represents 100% saturation. Since each argument requires 8 bits, this is known as a 24-bit colour model.

(c) The method setFromBar recovers the integer values represented by the three scroll bars. It then invokes setFromColor with an argument represented by these three integer values translated into a new colour object. The method setFromColor then sets the colour field to the given colour, sets the scroll bars to the integer values represented by this colour, and finally writes these values into the text field at the top of the window.

- Note that, in the example just described (i.e. when setFromColor is invoked by setFromBar), it is redundant for setFromColor to set the scroll bars since the colour it receives has been obtained from the same scroll bars! However, setFromColor is also invoked when the colour buttons are pressed (i.e. from the listeners BrightenButton and ColorButton), in which case it needs to reset the scroll bars.
- setFromBar is called only once by adjustmentValueChanged, which is called when the scroll bar is changed.

(d) The JPanel holds a grid of colour buttons and is therefore associated with a GridLayout manager via the statement:

```
p.setLayout (new GridLayout (4, 4, 3, 3));
```

- The add method associated with the GridLayout manager is used to add colour buttons to the grid.
- The default BorderLayout is used to place the panel and its buttons on the right-hand side (i.e. East) of the application window.

1.5 Exercises and solutions

[Remember to check whether an exercise from Budd, Chapter 13 is required for this year's TMA.]

Exercise 1.1

Describe one or two ways in which the Windows interface on your computer implements the following guidelines.

1 Consistency.

2 Displaying only the information that is relevant to the current context.

3 Deactivating commands that are inappropriate in the context of current actions.

You might also like to think about a problem that you have with your Windows interface, or any other Windows application that you run. Devise a guideline that would cover this.

Solution

1 *Consistency* The Windows system complies with this in the sense that the windows associated with most applications have the same look and feel, with similar menus providing similar functionality, similar mouse operations and key strokes, and similar help facilities. Run one application and you are well on the way to being able to use others.

2 *Displaying only relevant information* Again Windows has been designed to incorporate this guideline. For example, the use of menus means that if one wishes to edit some document, only the information appropriate to editing is displayed when one clicks on the editing menu.

3 *Deactivating commands* This is done in Windows. An example is in the Edit menu. If some text or figure has not been copied, the option to Paste is not available.

There are probably as many problems as there are people answering this question. Ours is a relatively simple one: it seems odd that to shut down the computer, you need to go to Start in order to choose Shut Down! This conflicts with an obvious guideline: *Operations should be found under intuitively-obvious menu headings.*

Exercise 1.2 (Exercise 2 in Budd, Chapter 13)

Write code to create a panel having a 2 × 2 grid layout with 3 pixels horizontal space and 5 pixels vertical space between components. Place buttons labelled 'one' to 'four' in the panels on the grid. Place this panel in the centre of your frame.

Solution

```
   // create new panel referenced by p
JPanel p = new JPanel ();
   // using GridLayout manager make a 2 x 2 grid with 3 and 5 pixels
   // between elements in the x and y directions, respectively,
p.setLayout (new GridLayout (2, 2, 3, 5));
   // add the buttons using the 'add' method from GridLayout manager
p.add (new JButton ("one"));
p.add (new JButton ("two"));
p.add (new JButton ("three"));
p.add (new JButton ("four"));
   // add the panel to the frame's content pane using the 'add' method
getContentPane ().add ("Center", p);
```

Exercise 1.3

In Subsection 13.3.2, Budd shows how an abstract class ButtonAdapter is developed. Like an interface, an abstract class has no instances, but sets out a specification for its subclasses (in this case, on how button listeners will behave). Unlike an interface, it can contain methods that already have an implementation. Since ButtonAdapter defines the way in which objects can be both buttons and listeners, it could have been used to define the class ColorButton. Show how this could be done.

Solution

A ColorButton class could have been defined from ButtonAdapter as follows.

```
private class ColorButton extends ButtonAdapter {
   private Color ourColor;

   public ColorButton (Color c, String name) {
      super (name);
      ourColor = c;
   }

   public void pressed () {
      setFromColor (ourColor);
   }
}
```

Note that actionPerformed is defined in the abstract class ButtonAdapter.

Exercise 1.4

In the ColorTest program, the quit-button facility is provided by an anonymous class. There are three ways to rewrite the program using a named class. Describe the three ways.

Solution

The three ways are as follows.

1. Define a separate listener class for a quit button. An example is QuitButtonListener, which implements ActionListener. A new button labelled 'Quit' then needs to be added to the panel and a new QuitButtonListener object added to the button.
2. Define a combined button-listener class for a quit button which, like ColorButton, both extends JButton and implements ActionListener. Then, add a new quit button to the panel in the same way that colour buttons are added.
3. Create a named class QuitButton by extending ButtonAdapter in the manner of the existing anonymous class as follows.

```
public class QuitButton extends ButtonAdapter {
    public QuitButton {
        super ("Quit");
    }
    public void pressed () {
        System.exit (0);
    }
}
```

   Then, in place of the existing statement containing the anonymous class, write the following statement.

```
p. add (new QuitButton ());
```

1.6 Summary of section

In this section you have learned to use more of the graphical components and layout managers available in the java.awt package and the javax.swing package. Before doing this you learned about some of the issues related to the HCI design. You were also introduced to anonymous classes.

Read the summary in Budd, Section 13.8.

2 APPLETS

There is little doubt that much of Java's growing popularity derives from its networking capabilities, in particular, its applet mechanism. Applets allow web browsers to execute applications, downloaded from other computers, in safety: that is, without compromising the safety of the client's machine. This section provides a brief introduction to applets.

2.1 Objectives

On completing this section you should be able to:

1 describe what an applet is and how it differs from the Java applications you have met so far in this unit;

2 run, under the control of your own Internet browser, a number of simple applets;

3 create and run your own simple applet.

2.2 Key terms and concepts

The important terms and concepts associated with this section are as follows.

JApplet	FlowLayout	URL
applet	HTML	web browser
applet tag (HTML)	java.applet package	web page
code (HTML)	parameter tag (HTML)	web server
codebase (HTML)	security (applet)	World Wide Web (the Web)

2.3 Study activities

So far you have met most of the important mechanisms used in Java for writing applications although some, such as concurrency and exceptions, will be explored in more depth in Blocks 2 and 3. You have also learned how to browse and use Java packages like java.io, javax.swing, and java.awt. In this section, you will be introduced to facilities of the java.applet, java.awt and javax.swing package especially those relating to applets.

The most important class in this section is the Swing class JApplet. This class inherits from the applet class that was used in Java 1.1; that is, java.applet.Applet.

1 Do the practical activity in Section 7 of the *IDE Handbook*.

2 Read Budd, Chapter 21 up to the end of Section 21.3. You will see that Budd uses the PaintApplet as the main teaching example, which is why it is essential that you have followed the steps in the practical activity in Section 7 of the *IDE Handbook* before reading the chapter.

3 While Budd, Sections 21.4 and 21.5 are not part of this course, you may like to read them if you have the time.

4 At the end of each section of Budd, Chapter 21, attempt the relevant SAQ (labelled with the same number as the section of Budd).

5 Finally, when you have completed the above, attempt the exercises in Subsection 2.5 and check whether any further exercises from Budd, Chapter 21 are included in the TMA for this unit.

Explanatory notes

1 The need for a web server (Budd, Section 21.2)

In Exercise 2.1 in Subsection 2.5, you are asked to access the M301 web site to view an applet in action. This is possible because the OU computer that supports our web page is a web server. That is, it executes a continuously running program, known as a server that responds to requests from your computer running a program, known as a client. You will learn about client–server programming in *Unit 3.2*.

2 The `<param>` tag and the `getParameter ()` method (Budd, Section 21.1)

The HTML document can contain any number of `<param>` tags, each one of which has the general form shown in Budd, Section 21.1 as follows:

```
<param name=soundSource value="audio">
```

where the name of the parameter (`soundsource`) and its value (`"audio"`) are specified by the programmer. The applet can access these values via the `getParameter` method (a member of the `Applet` class). This method has a single argument (the name of the parameter) and returns a string (the value of the parameter). For example,

```
String s = getParameter (soundsource);
```

would assign the string `"audio"` to the variable `s`.

2.4 SAQs and solutions

All study questions are from Budd, Chapter 21.

SAQ 21.1

(a) What is an applet?(Study Question 1)

(b) What is html? (Study Question 2)

(c) How can a web page be made to point to an applet? (Study Question 3)

(d) What happens if a web browser cannot load and execute an applet described by an `applet` tag? (Study Question 5).

(e) What is contained within the `<applet>` tag of `PaintApplet.htm which you create using the applet wizard in folder C:\JavaProjects\Applets\src`? What information does this tag convey?

Solution

(a) An **applet** is a program written for the World Wide Web (the Web) and executed under the control of a *web browser*. A 'pointer' to the executable applet code is embedded in a *web page*. Depending upon the applet developer's intention, the applet code will be executed by a web browser either automatically when the page is accessed by the web browser or when its user decides to execute it directly (e.g. by double clicking on its icon).

(b) **HTML** stands for HyperText Markup Language. It is a language for constructing web pages. File names that use either an `.html` or an `.htm` extension indicate that the files contain HTML code.

(c) A web page can be made to refer to an applet by including, within the `<applet>` tag, information about:

- the URL of the applet using the clause `codeBase=` ... . This clause can be omitted, in which case the URL of the current document is used. The URL must refer to the directory containing the applet, not the applet file itself.
- the name of the file containing the applet code using the clause `code=` ... .
- the size of the applet, in pixels, using the clauses `width=` ... and `height=` ... .

(d) If an applet cannot be loaded (perhaps it is no longer at the location specified in the HTML document), any text between <applet> and </applet>, which is not part of a <param> clause, will be displayed by the browser. It is good practice always to include such text to alert the user.

(e) The applet tag is:

```
<APPLET
CODEBASE = "."
CODE     = "PaintApplet.class"
NAME     = "TestApplet"
WIDTH    = 400
HEIGHT   = 300
HSPACE   = 0
VSPACE   = 0
ALIGN    = middle
>
</APPLET>
```

This informs the browser that an applet is to be executed, the code for which can be found in the file PaintApplet.class on the local machine in the same directory as the html file (indicated by CODEBASE = "."). and that the output from the applet should be displayed in an area of the browser window, which is 300 pixels in height by 400 pixels in width. (Note that inside a JBuilder project the html and class files need not reside in the same directory, but they must do so when they are to be shown in a web browser with the CODEBASE given above. If you moved the .class files to a directory C:\MyClasses the codebase line would need to be altered to CODEBASE = "C:\MyClasses").

SAQ 21.2

Why is there a security issue with applets and how has it been addressed?

Solution

Applets are a threat to security because they have the potential to cause significant damage to client machines when executed. Therefore, applets are restricted in what they can do when compared to ordinary applications.

SAQ 21.3

List the main differences between the Paint application (see Budd, Figures 18.5 and 18.6) and the PaintApplet.
(See the code file C:\JavaProjects\Applets\src\PaintApplet.java.)

Solution

The main differences are as follows.

The top-level class extends JApplet rather than JFrame. This has two important effects:

- it turns the top-level class into an object of type JPanel rather than a window;
- it enables the application to inherit the four required applet operations: init, start, stop and destroy, which can be used as they are or overridden.

The applet does not have a main method.

In place of the constructor for the application, the applet uses the method init. In the case of PaintApplet, init has been overridden to provide similar facilities to those given by the constructor for Paint.

The fact that the applet is a panel rather than a window, means that there are some minor differences between the application and the applet:

- panels do not have titles;
- the size of the panel is set by the `<APPLET>` tag in the HTML document rather than in the applet itself;
- a panel has a `FlowLayout` manager by default, so it has been necessary to reset this to border layout in order to place the buttons in a similar position to the application.

SAQ 21.4 (OPTIONAL)

How can information be passed from an HTML document to an applet?

Solution

Any information placed in a `<param>` tag can be accessed by an applet via the `getParameter` method (a member of the `Applet` class).

2.5 Exercises and solutions

[Remember to check whether an exercise from Budd, Chapter 21 is required for this year's TMA.]

Exercise 2.1

Consult the web page for this unit and click on the Cannon game applet hyperlink. Describe what happens.

Solution

You should see a web page which contains an applet that implements the second version of the cannon game that you studied in *Unit 1.2*, which allows you to interactively set the angle of the cannon and fire it.

Exercise 2.2

Produce the same web page that you saw in Exercise 2.1 by carrying out the following steps.

1. Using 1–3 of Practical Activity 7.1 of the *IDE Handbook* as a guide, create a new applet project called `CannonApplet` in the folder `JavaProjects\Applets`.
2. Name the resulting new applet class `CannonWorld` (use step 4 of Practical Activity 7.1 in the *IDE Handbook* as a guide).
3. Modify the contents of your new `CannonWorld` applet class so that it provides the same functionality as the class in `JavaProjects\Cannons\src\CannonWorld.java`.
4. The statement that starts and keeps the original `CannonWorld` game running is

   ```
   while (true) world.run ();
   ```

   in the `main` method of the class. To provide the same functionality in the applet, the applet's `start` method (see Budd, Section 21.3) must be overridden to include the statement

   ```
   while (true) run ();
   ```

   (Note that unlike the `CannonWorld` application, the `CannonWorld` applet does not use a `world` object.)
5. Update the automatically generated HTML file for the applet (i.e. `CannonWorld.html`), so that the values for `FrameHeight` and `FrameWidth` are the same as those in the `CannonWorld.java` file.
6. Don't forget to include in your applet project all the other files that are required for the `CannonWorld` game (see Exercise 4.1 of the *IDE Handbook*).

Solution

You can find a copy of our solution to this problem in the folder:

C:\JavaProjects\Exercises\Cannon\src

2.6 Summary of section

In this section you have learned how to develop simple web pages and applets, and how to run applets using a web browser.

Read the summary in Budd, Section 21.6.

3 INPUT AND OUTPUT STREAMS

We shall use the convention that the computer on which the applet is stored is called its *home* machine, and the computer on which it is executed is called its *host* machine. In general, an applet will be downloaded via the Internet from its home machine to be executed on the host machine.

You learned how to use Java applets in the last section. Although applets enhance the capabilities for developing web pages for the Internet, they need not necessarily involve programs that make use of networking facilities. For example, the `Paint` applet that you used when learning about applets simply uses the Java programming resources it found on the host machine on which it was being run. However, more sophisticated applets can be developed which will draw on the resources (other web pages, files, databases, etc.) from its own home machine. To do this it needs to use:

- the stream facilities provided in the package java.io for inputting and outputting data;
- the networking facilities provided in the package java.net.

This section will introduce you to the stream facilities in java.io.

3.1 Objectives

On completing this section you should be able to:

1. describe the structure of the classes in the java.io package that provide the facilities to input and output data;
2. use the facilities of the java.io package to read data from, and write data to, various kinds of sources and destinations respectively;
3. use the facilities of the java.io package that support the communication between sources and sinks.

3.2 Key terms and concepts

The important terms and concepts associated with this section are as follows.

binary representation	Reader/Writer streams	stream
byte	sink	textual representation
input/output streams	source	Unicode

3.3 Study activities

The work of this section is aimed at supporting the network programming that you will learn in Block 3. The use of streams as a mechanism for transferring data between two executing programs is crucial in enabling clients and servers to communicate with each other across a network.

Before reading about the stream classes in Budd, it will be helpful to discuss the main terms associated with the communication of data in Java.

1. **Byte** This is normally the smallest grouping of bits (8 of them) used by a computer to represent data. For example, 10101010 is representative of a typical byte.
2. **Binary representation** This refers to the way in which a particular type of data is represented in a computer. For example, the primitive data type `int` in Java represents integers that can be stored in four bytes (e.g. 00000000,00000000,00000000,01100001 = 97), integers of type `short` use two bytes, floating-point values are held in four bytes, and so on. Characters have traditionally been coded in a number of different ways. The ASCII character set, used by many computers over many years, uses 1 byte to represent a character (e.g. 01100001 = 'a'). However, this means that only 256 different characters can be represented by this code. In order to internationalize the character set, so that

We have used commas to separate the bytes for legibility purposes; they would not appear in the binary representation.

- characters from other languages can be incorporated, a new character code called *Unicode* has been developed which uses two bytes to represent each character. The binary representation of 'a' in this code is now 00000000,01100001. This makes it possible to represent 2^{16} (or 65 536) characters. The ASCII code forms the first 256 characters of Unicode.
- It is interesting to note that the binary representation of the `short` integer 97, 00000000,01100001, is the same as the Unicode for 'a'. This raises the issue of how a given collection of bytes is to be interpreted. In typed languages like Java, this is always made clear using typed declarations. That is, if certain memory locations are associated with a variable, the type of the variable determines how the bytes should be interpreted.

3 **Textual representation** This refers to the symbolic notation that we understand, and not the *binary representation* that computers use. So when writing 'a' or '97' to the terminal, a conversion must be made from their binary representation to the textual representation that we will understand. Note also that, since the binary representation of 'a' of type `char` is the same as that of the integer '97' of type `short`, it must also be made clear whether it is a character or an integer which is being represented. As noted in 2 above, this is always made clear in Java using typed declarations.

4 **Sources** and **sinks** *Sources* of data are the places/devices from which data is fetched. Common sources are files, the keyboard, byte arrays in memory, string buffers, and so on. *Sinks* (or *destinations*) represent places/devices to which data is sent. As well as being sources, files, byte arrays and string buffers can also be sinks. The screen is also a sink.

5 **Stream** This represents a programming abstraction and can be thought of as a communication channel between the program and a source (an input stream) or sink (an output stream). It will come as no surprise to learn that this channel is represented as an object in a Java program, and has associated with it various methods for sending, receiving and manipulating data.

Fundamentally, a stream is a flow of one or more bytes. However, as you will learn below, Java provides classes that enable you to interpret this data not only as individual bytes but also as the binary representation of other data types like integers, characters, strings, and so on. For example, by taking two bytes at a time, a stream of bytes can be interpreted as a stream of Unicode characters or a stream of short integers. These classes also provide the facilities to indicate when a textual representation is required; for example, when outputting to a terminal or printer. So, for example, when inputting data (bytes) from a text file, special streams are available to 'read' these bytes in the form of one or other of the Java data types.

1 Read Budd, Chapter 14, Sections 14.1–14.4 and 14.7. Read the explanatory notes, if any, relevant to each section.
2 At the end of each section of Budd, Chapter 14 attempt the relevant SAQ (labelled with the same number as the section of Budd).
3 Finally, when you have completed the above, attempt the exercises in Subsection 3.5 and check whether any other exercises from Budd, Chapter 14 are included in the TMA for this unit.

Explanatory notes

1 Input and output streams work with bytes (Budd, Section 14.1)

The `InputStream` and `OutputStream` classes are the basic classes in Java for dealing with byte streams. They provide objects that can be connected to various sources and sinks, and provide the methods that enable data of various types to be read from, or written to, these sources or sinks. So, for example, if data were to be read from a file (i.e. an array of bytes held on disk), a `FileInputStream` object would be created and associated, through its constructor, with the file in question. The methods of

FileInputStream, inherited from InputStream, would then be available to read and manipulate the data from the file in various ways.

2 Reader and writer streams work with Unicode characters (Budd, Section 14.1)

The Reader and Writer classes are a newer set of classes, which have been designed to work with character streams. In other words, these classes view the bytes associated with a stream as though they are a stream of Unicode (i.e. two-byte) characters. These classes have been designed to overcome some of the inconsistencies that can occur when dealing with this new character set using the byte stream classes. Once you have learned the principles of InputStream and OutputStream, using the Reader and Writer classes is quite straightforward.

3 The use of the term 'stream' (Budd, Section 14.1)

In Budd and this course text, the term 'stream' is often used in two ways. In general, it means a communication channel between the program and a source or sink as described above. However, in another context, it is frequently used to refer to the InputStream/OutputStream classes as distinct from the Reader/Writer classes. The context should usually make clear which meaning is intended.

4 PushBackInputStream example (Budd, Subsection 14.2.2)

The PushBackInputStream can unread a single character. Budd mentions the example of the textual representation of a numeric value, such as 456. The input stream might be as follows:

```
456 as entry.
```

After the '6' has been read, a space is read. At that point, it is realized that the space should not be part of the number. Thus the space, as a single character, is pushed back into the input stream to be read later.

3.4 SAQs and solutions

'Study Questions' are from Budd, Chapter 14.

SAQ 14.1

(a) What are the various ways in which the following byte array can be interpreted?

00000000	00000000	00000000	01100001
0	1	2	3

(b) What is the difference between the *stream* class hierarchies and the *Reader/Writer* hierarchies? (Study Question 1)

Solution

(a) The four bytes can be read as

- four separate bytes;
- two Unicode characters of two bytes each with the first two bytes being the binary representation of 'null' and the next two 'a';
- two short integers of two bytes each with the first two bytes being the binary representation of '0' (zero) and the next two '97';
- one integer of type int consisting of four bytes, which is the binary representation of '97'.
- a number of type float, which also has a binary representation of four bytes.

(b) The *stream* classes are based on bytes (8-bit quantities) whereas the Reader/Writer classes manipulate two-byte (character) values.

SAQ 14.2

(a) Describe the methods that are common to all subclasses of InputStream. (Study Question 2)

(b) What are the different types of physical locations from which an input stream can be read? (Study Question 3)

(c) Describe how a FilterInputStream combines both inheritance and composition. (Study Question 4)

(d) What is the difference between the InputStream class and the DataInputStream class? (Study Question 5)

Solution

(a) The methods common to all subclasses of InputStream are those inherited from InputStream. Budd describes the following main methods (there are others).

- read () reads a single byte from the input and returns it as a positive int (or –1 if the end of the stream was reached). This method will wait until data is available to be read. That is, the program that is executing will be blocked (stopped from executing) until the data is available to be read.
- read (byte [ ] buffer) reads a collection of values from the input, placing them into a byte array here named buffer, and returns a positive int containing the number of bytes read or –1 if the end of the stream was reached.
- skip (long n) skips n bytes from the input and returns a long value containing a count of the number of bytes that were actually skipped.
- available () determines the number of bytes readable without blocking and returns it as an int.
- close () closes the input stream.

(b) The physical locations (or sources) from which an input stream can be read are:

- byte array;
- file;
- pipe (a buffered data area used for both reading and writing).

(c) You have already dealt with a similar question of combining inheritance with composition in SAQ 10.4 of *Unit 1.4*, Subsection 1.4. FilterInputStream *is-a* InputStream because it inherits from InputStream, but also *has-a* InputStream by virtue of composition.

(d) InputStream is an abstract class that specifies the common methods that will be provided by all its subclasses. In particular, it provides the basic methods to read bytes from a source either singly or as an array. DataInputStream *is-a* InputStream and therefore implements all its methods. However, it also *has-a* InputStream. This means that it is a wrapper class providing additional functionality for reading an input stream. In the case of DataInputStream, its additional methods enable an input stream to be read as one or other of the binary representations of various Java data types.

SAQ 14.3

What task is performed by a StreamTokenizer?(Study Question 7)

Solution

StreamTokenizer provides facilities to break a textual file into single tokens, such as words and numbers.

SAQ 14.4

(a) What is the purpose of the method flush in both output stream and writer abstractions? (Study Question 8)

(b) Describe the different targets to which an output stream can write. (Study Question 9)

Solution

(a) Outputting data to a device one byte/character at a time is an inefficient process. Many subclasses of OutputStream (and Writer as well) will collect data in an internal buffer and only send it to the device when enough has been collected for it to be done efficiently. On occasions, however, the programmer may wish to force the stream to output what is currently in the buffer. The method flush is used to do this.

(b) The targets of an output stream can be:

- byte array;
- file;
- pipe.

SAQ 14.7

How are readers and writers linked to streams? (Study Question 12)

(Note, in talking about streams, Budd is referring to the classes associated with InputStream and OutputStream — see explanatory note 3 above.)

Solution

Readers and writers are linked to streams via the wrapper classes InputStreamReader and OutputStreamReader respectively. For example, the constructor for InputStreamReader takes an InputStream object as an argument and returns an object that responds to Reader methods. Similarly, the constructor for OutputStreamReader takes an OutputStream object as an argument and returns an object that responds to Writer methods.

3.5 Exercises and solutions

[Remember to check whether an exercise from Budd, Chapter 14 is required for this year's TMA.]

Exercise 3.1

Write the Java code that would create a BufferedReader object, inRead, from an InputStream object inS.

Solution

The long way would be to do it in two stages. First, create an InputStreamReader object linking an input stream to a reader as follows:

```
InputStreamReader r = new InputStreamReader (inS);
```

(Note that

```
Reader r = new InputStreamReader (inS);
```

would also be acceptable since the new InputStream object being created *is-a* Reader object).

Second, wrap r into a BufferedReader object as follows:

```
BufferedRead inRead = new BufferedReader (r);
```

A shorter way is to combine both these steps as follows:

```
BufferedReader inRead = new BufferedReader (new InputStreamReader (inS));
```

Exercise 3.2

Exercise 1 in Budd, Chapter 14 reads:

> Create a new subclass of FilterInputStream that reads values from an input stream and converts all uppercase characters to lowercase. How would you test your program?

Do this exercise by creating a new project named ConvertCaps, and completing the classes in the files ConvertCaps.java and ConvertCapsInputStream.java which can be found in the directory C:\JavaProjects\Exercises\Caps\src. Both files contain hints on how to proceed.

You will have to create two new text files:

```
C:\Temp\JavaFiles\UandLcase.txt
C:\Temp\JavaFiles\Lcase.txt
```

by copying the two files UandLcase.txt and Lcase.txt from the directory C:\JavaProjects\Exercises\Caps\src into the directory C:\Temp\JavaFiles. The former contains some text that includes both upper- and lower-case letters. The latter file should be empty. The result of running the program will be to copy the contents of UandLcase.txt to Lcase.txt with all upper-case characters converted to lower case.

In the file ConvertCaps.java the following string appears: "C:\\Temp\\JavaFiles\\UandLcase.txt". In a string, the character '\' is known as an escape character and influences the meaning of the character that immediately follows it. For example, the combination '\n' stands for the newline character. The combination '\\' that appears in ConvertCaps.java stands for the single character '\'. See Budd, Appendix A.3.1.

The method readLine(), from the class DataInputStream, reads characters from the stream until it encounters a newline character, a carriage return character, or a newline-carriage return pair. The returned string does not include the newline or carriage return character.

It is necessary to ensure that the file Lcase.txt which is put into the folder Temp\JavaFiles is NOT read-only. To do this right click on the file, select Properties and make sure that the box marked Read-only is not ticked. Another point to note about the exercise is that the two versions of ConvertCaps (the one you are asked to complete, and the other provided as a solution) contain different ways of creating the variable fileOut, namely:

```
PrintStream fileOut = new PrintStream (
                      new FileOutputStream (toFileName));
```

in Solution_ConvertCaps.java and

```
PrintStream fileOut = new PrintStream (
                      new FileOutputStream (
                      new File(toFileName)));
```

in ConvertCaps.java.

This was unintentional. However the result is the same. The first version uses a constructor for FileOuputStream that takes the name of the file as a string argument. The second version uses a constructor for FileOutputStream that takes a File object directly (this file object is created from the string containing the file name using the appropriate constructor of File objects).

Finally, a technical point that you can ignore at this stage if you wish. ConvertCapsInputStream extends FilterInputStream and overrides its read method so that, in reading an upper case letter, it is converted to the equivalent lower case one. The read method that is imported throws an exception, so the overridden method must also throw an exception. As you will see in the solution, the following code appears inside the overridden read method.

```
try {
  byteVal = in.read();
} catch (IOException e) {System.exit(0);}
```

Even though in.read can throw an exception, enclosing it in a try statement is not strictly necessary. This is because in.read occurs within the body of the redefined read method which, because it throws an exception, must itself be invoked within a try statement. This 'outer' level try statement would also serve to catch an exception stemming from in.read. (See Budd, Chapter 22.2 where this issue is discussed in relation to the DateServer constructor.)

Solution

A specimen solution is contained in the files Solution_ConvertCaps.java and Solution_ConvertCapsInputStream.java, which can be found in the directory C:\JavaProjects\Exercises\Caps\src. To run these files you will need to remove the prefix Solution_ from the file names and add the files to a new project. The solution files also contain additional comments on the code.

3.6 Summary of section

Read the summary in Budd, Section 14.8.

4 SUMMARY OF THE UNIT

In this unit you have:

- learned about writing user interfaces employing Swing classes;
- learned how to write applets;
- learned about the stream classes in *java.io*.

Read the summaries in Budd, Sections 13.8, 14.8 and 21.6.

INDEX